# Local
# planning

# Local planning

**SEBASTIAN LOEW**

*Lecturer, Polytechnic of the South Bank, London*

PEMBRIDGE PRESS LTD

First published 1979 by Pembridge Press Ltd
16 Pembridge Road  London W11  UK
Set in 10/11 pt Theme by Allset and
printed and bound in the UK by
Redwood Burn Ltd of Trowbridge and Esher
Copyright © 1979 by Sebastian Loew

ISBN: 0-86206-000-1

# CONTENTS

### List of tables

144961

# LIST OF FIGURES

# ACKNOWLEDGEMENTS

A few years ago, I started teaching local planning to students preparing for Part 4 of the Royal Town Planning Institute Final Examination. I discovered that there was no text available upon which to base my lectures. That was the first stimulus to write this book. It would not have become a reality had it not been for the students with whom I discussed and tested most of the ideas contained in the text. My colleagues at the Polytechnic of the South Bank provided the encouragement I needed to write the book and though I cannot name them all, I am indebted to them, particularly those who, like Rob Anderson and Dave Frost, criticised and commented upon my original drafts.

I would also like to acknowledge the inspiration and stimulation I received from a number of authors and from all the local plans published by local authorities throughout the country. I am especially grateful to those authorities which have allowed me to reproduce material from their published plans.

Finally I would like to thank John Copland for checking my typescript.

*Sebastian Loew*
*May 1979*

# GLOSSARY OF TERMS

ACTION AREA:  An area indicated in the structure plan (qv) for comprehensive treatment by development, redevelopment or improvement within ten years.  (Town & Country Planning Act 1971.)

ACTIVITY RATE:  Proportion of the population which is economically active, ie in employment or seeking employment.

BETTERMENT:  Increased value of a piece of land as a result of central or local government action, whether positive or negative.  (Uthwatt Committee Report 1942.)

CALL IN:  Certain proposals, by private or public developers, which the Secretary of State regards as too important to be dealt with at local authority level, can be 'called in' for his decision.  (Town & Country Planning Act 1971.)

CASH FLOW:  The getting and spending of money, the circulation or streaming of money both into and out of a business.

COMPREHENSIVE DEVELOPMENT AREA:  The complete development or redevelopment of a sizeable area as a phased operation in accordance with a comprehensive plan for the whole area.  (Town & Country Planning Acts 1944 & 47.)

CONSERVATION AREA:  Area designated by a local authority to protect and enhance its character.  Often includes buildings of architectural or historical interest.  Redevelopment is not excluded but has to be in keeping with area's character.  (Civic Amenities Act 1967, Town & Country Planning (Amendment) Act 1972.)

CONVENIENCE GOODS:  Those goods purchased for immediate or short-term consumption, eg food items, toiletries, hardware, as opposed to 'durable goods'.

COST-BENEFIT STUDY:  The analysis of possible alternatives involving different levels of expenditure and differing degrees of benefit, in order to decide which one to choose.

DENSITY (RESIDENTIAL):  The number of people or amount of accommodation per unit of land, eg people per acre, rooms per hectare. 'Gross residential density' includes ancillary uses such as schools or public open spaces.

DENSITY (COMMERCIAL):  See 'Plot ratio'.

9

DISTRICT PLAN: A type of local plan prepared for the whole or part of the planning authority's area where detailed planning matters need to be studied and set out in a comprehensive way. (Regulation 15-1.)

DWELLING: Building or part of a building designed for the occupation of a single family household as a temporary or permanent home.

ENUMERATION DISTRICT: Area assigned to one enumerator on Census day. Each ED consists of approximately 150 households in towns and 50 households in the country.

ENVIRONMENTAL AREA: An area having no extraneous traffic, and within which considerations of environment predominate over the use of vehicles. (Traffic in Towns Report.)

EQUITY SHARE (also called 'Ordinary share'): A share in the capital of an undertaking, on which the return fluctuates according to the profits available for distribution after prior claims have been met.

GENERAL IMPROVEMENT AREA: Residential area designated by a housing authority, in which improvements are made to the environment and grants given for the improvement of housing. (Housing Acts 1969 and 1974.)

GENTRIFICATION: A phenomenon typical of inner-city areas, where working class families living in relatively cheap property are replaced by wealthier middle-class families.

GREEN BELT: A girdle of open country surrounding a town or conurbation, in which there are limitations on outward growth.

HOLDING COMPANY: In certain circumstances, a company can be a subsidiary of another company. The latter is known as the holding company. (Companies Act 1948.)

HOUSEHOLD: Consists of a group of individuals who share living quarters and their principal meals. Generally a single family but it can include other people. (A definition is given by the Census of Population, but it has tended to vary from one census to another.)

HOUSING ACTION AREA: Residential area designated by a housing authority because the living conditions are unsatisfactory and can be improved within a period of 5 years, for the benefit of the inhabitants, mainly via improvement grants. (Housing Act 1974.)

MULTIPLE OCCUPATION: A dwelling which is occupied by more than one household is said to be multi-occupied (Housing Act 1969). This expression is equivalent to that of 'sharing' which in the Census of Population includes not only the sharing of a room, but also that of facilities (eg a WC or even a staircase).

NON-CONFORMING USE: An activity taking place on land zoned for another use. It mainly, though not exclusively, refers to industry located in a residential zone.

OVERCROWDING: Occurs whenever the number of persons occupying a dwelling becomes higher than can be accommodated satisfactorily. In
10

Britain at present, it is considered to be upwards of 1.5 person per room. Under-occupation is the other extreme, ie a dwelling which is excessively large for the number of inhabitants.

PLOT RATIO: Measure of commercial density (see 'Density'). Total floor space per plot area excluding local access roads.

RAT RUN: Local road used only when congestion diverts traffic from the more direct main roads.

SALE AND LEASEBACK: A transaction whereby a capital-raising owner sells his property to an investment-minded purchaser, who then grants the vendor a lease of it.

SEMIOTICS: A general philosophical theory of signs and symbols that deals especially with their function in both artificially constructed and natural language.

SLEEPING POLICEMAN: A constructed hump in the road that forces cars to slow down.

SOCIO-ECONOMIC GROUPS: The Census classifies economically active persons into 17 categories according to their jobs' social and economic status. Managers are in SEG 1, semi-skilled manual workers in SEG 10.

SQUATTER: A person who without licence occupies land to which he has no legal title and for which he pays no rent.

STATUTORY UNDERTAKERS: Bodies which by statute have a duty to provide a certain service for the public at large; generally nationalised industries such as the Central Electricity Generating Board, the Gas Council, British Rail, etc.

STRUCTURE PLAN: Primarily a written statement of policy accompanied by diagrams. It deals with broad land-use policies and with the management of traffic. To be prepared by county authorities and approved by the Secretary of State. (Town & Country Planning Act 1971.)

SUBJECT PLAN: Type of local plan designed to enable detailed treatment to be given to a particular description of development or land-use, eg minerals or footpaths. (Regulation 15-3.)

TENURE: Related to ownership of housing; a distinction is usually made between housing rented from a public authority or a private landlord (either furnished or unfurnished), or owned by the occupier (either absolutely or as a mortgagor). Landlord-tenant relationship.

ULTRA VIRES; Beyond the powers of. Any action which goes beyond the powers given to local authorities by Acts of Parliament would be voidable as 'ultra vires'.

USE CLASSES (ORDER): Prescribes classes of use within which changes may take place without constituting development. Changes of use from one class to another do constitute development and require planning permission. (Town & Country Planning Act 1971.)

WARD: Administrative division which elects a councillor. Used in the Census of Population for aggregation of data.

# INTRODUCTION

The expression 'Local Plan' was introduced by the report of the Planning Advisory Group, *The future of development plans* in 1965 (1), and officially incorporated into British planning legislation by the 1968 Town & Country Planning Act. (2) The concept of local planning is, however, much older than this legislation, and the expression has been used in a wide sense, probably meaning different things to different people.

Since the introduction of the new planning system in 1968, and particularly since the reform of local government in 1974, a multiplicity of interpretations has been given regarding what local plans are for, the form they should take, how they should be prepared, etc. (3) A review of the activities of the London boroughs for example, gives an indication of the wide variety of documents that can be produced under the label 'local plan'—from informal plans for small areas to statutory documents for a whole borough. Taking the view that it was not its role to intervene, the Department of the Environment has failed until recently, to give clear directions of what it expects local authorities to produce. In February 1978 the Department circulated a note to local authorities containing advice which, no doubt, reflected its reactions to the examination of a number of submitted local plans. (4)

Ten years after the incorporation of the 1968 Act into the statute-book, the enthusiasm that hailed it has been replaced by some cynicism, doubt and a lot of questioning. A number of articles have been written about local planning, mainly recounting experiences gained through being involved in the preparation of plans. Some have criticised or given opinions about the process or the way the legislation is applied. Lately, a large number of local plans are being published, mostly as draft documents, sometimes as adopted 'informal' plans, and, in a few cases, as final statutorily-adopted documents. Up to now however, no text has attempted to encompass the experience obtained, perhaps because the field is so vast and has so many ramifications. This book attempts to deal with the subject in a relatively narrow context—that of the British town-planning system—but within it, various approaches and various kinds of plans will be considered.

The book starts by examining the legislative framework and the various

13

stages of planning practice at the local level. This is followed by discussion of a number of issues which are particularly relevant to the practitioner working on local plans and are related to other professions with whom town-planners interact. The last part of the book deals with particular kinds of local plans, with a dominant land-use or a specific problem. A substantial part of the analysis is based on plans published in the last few years.

The book is intended to offer an introduction to local planning; it is addressed to all those interested in the environment, and primarily, to students of town-planning and to other related professions such as architecture and estate management. It should also be of interest to those professionally or politically involved in the preparation of local plans, as well as to the layman involved in a battle with the local council. Though it is too early to review the long-range effects of the new planning system, or to give an insight into the political aspects of the process, the text should guide future analyses. Wherever relevant, the differences between ideal situations, the spirit of the legislation and the realities of daily practice are indicated.

## Definitions

The *Oxford English dictionary* gives the following definition of 'local': 'Of place, belonging or peculiar to some place'.

From this, it could be concluded that local plans deal with the planning of a place—which is true, but does not explain the difference from structure-planning or any other kind of planning related to places, albeit different ones. Professionals in Britain talk about 'local plans' as opposed to 'structure plans' and presumably have images of these two kinds of plans; but how to define exactly what local planning deals with seems less clear.

The Royal Town Planning Institute's *Examinations handbook* states:

'The spatial range of planning has been subdivided into four fields for the purpose of the examination: local, urban and metropolitan, regional and natural resources.'

Later, it defines the local planning field:

'This field is concerned with the smallest systems of land-use or settlement, and operates, for example, at the spatial scale of a village, a neighbourhood, an urban area ripe for comprehensive redevelopment, an industrial estate or a precinct of special character or activity.' (5)

It is debatable whether this subdivision of the environment in spatial scales and the definitions given correspond to any reality, or are purely arbitrary. Local planning seems to embrace a wide variety of types and sizes of areas, and it would be difficult to pinpoint what the 'smallest systems of land-use' should be, whether a one-plot development or a town centre. It will be seen later that one form of statutory plan is not even specifically related to an area.

The guiding hand of the new planning system, the *Development plans manual* states that local plans 'will be concerned with more detailed implementation of the policies and proposals of the structure plan. Local plans will cover small areas and large and they will deal with many different aspects of planning.' (6)

It appears that size and location are not the defining criteria of local plans; rather are they a certain level of detail and, I would add, comprehensiveness and implementation in a fairly limited period of time.

### Why have local plans?

The necessity for and the acceptance of local plans stem from a combination of practical and ideological considerations. It is part of the current socio-political trends of western societies to aim at some degree of devolution from the centre to local communities. Whether this is accepted as a genuine desire to encourage increased civic involvement, or is considered a gimmick on the part of the establishment, a number of countries have started to implement policies which allow a certain amount of local decision-making, and accept the fact that planning has to be done with local people and not for them by remote bureaucrats.

Following a different ideological stream is the belief in the interaction of men and environment, which permeates the town-planning profession; this leads to the concept of plans specifically based on land-uses, physically orientated. Conversely, if the point of view that society is not affected by environmental considerations was accepted, locally based problems would be of lesser relevance; social inter-relationships would not necessarily be place-based, a concept which goes against most philosophical notions of town-planning.

On a more practical level, the introduction within the British planning system of the structure-plan containing only general policy guidelines led almost directly to the need for additional indications of how development would take place on the ground. If town-planning is to have a role in shaping the environment, developers must be given an idea of what is expected of them, what they will be allowed to do and what restrictions will be imposed on them. This kind of guidance is not to be found in general or abstract documents; neither can development control be effective without a firm basis for decision-making.

From another perspective, local planning, albeit under different names, has been the basis of various studies of society, urban and rural alike. Sociologists, in particular, have looked at fairly well-defined neighbourhoods to analyse changes in society, relationships between various groups, conflict, leadership patterns, etc; in other words, they have used the local area as a laboratory from which generalisations—sometimes erroneous—about the functioning of society, have been deduced. The work of such authors as Park and Burgess and their followers of the Chicago School is

15

based on the idea that humans find their natural area according to various socio-economic characteristics; and whether this concept is accepted or rejected, it remains a basis for study of urban society which is still current today. (7) The logical conclusion from such studies is that planning can and should be done at local level.

## REFERENCES

1  Ministry of Housing and Local Government (MOHLG), *The future of development plans*, a report by the Planning Advisory Group, HMSO, London, 1965.

2  Town and Country Planning Act 1968, c72, HMSO, London, 1968.

3  Local Government Act 1972, c70, HMSO, London, 1972.  The implementation of the Act in England and Wales took effect on April 1st 1974, with the creation of the present system of counties and districts.

4  Department of the Environment, Local Plans Note 1/78, Form and Content of Local Plans, February 1978.  These notes are not for general consumption: they are sent by the DOE to all planning authorities, but lesser mortals do not necessarily have access to them.

5  The Royal Town Planning Institute, *Examinations handbook 1974*, Final examinations syllabus, Part III and IV, p20.

6  MOHLG, *Development plans, a manual of form and content*, HMSO, London, 1970.

7  R E Park, *Human communities*, Free Press, Chicago, 1955.
   E W Burgess, *Urban sociology*, University of Chicago Press, 1964.
   For a further discussion of the Chicago School, see for instance
J R Mellor, *Urban sociology in an urbanised society*, Routledge and Kegan Paul, London, 1977.

Chapter 1

# LEGISLATIVE BACKGROUND

## Local plans before 1965

The various definitions of local plans mentioned in the Introduction encompass more than the 1968 legislation's local plans. A variety of other local plans existed before, and some cases still exist outside the framework of the post-1968 Acts. A brief review of some of these may be useful to an understanding of the directions in which local planning has developed more recently.

Before the second world war, planning was entirely local in that there were no statutory plans covering anything but specific areas of limited size. Local authorities were entitled (and in certain cases obliged) to prepare planning schemes indicating merely the land-use zoning of these areas. Since these schemes in most cases reflected what was happening on the ground, they were not set into a wider framework or backed by an elaborate survey or a discussion of the aims of the plan. Their importance now is principally historical and they need not be considered here any further. (1)

### Comprehensive development areas

With the 1947 Town & Country Planning Act the planning duties and powers of local authorities were greatly widened. The whole country was to be covered by 'development plans', indicating how each local authority's area was to be developed. (2) Among the documents that could be included with the development plans were the Comprehensive Development Areas plans, already introduced by the 1944 Act (3), which were for areas that the local planning authority considered should be developed or redeveloped for any of the following reasons:
  (i) to deal satisfactorily with extensive war damage,
 (ii) to deal satisfactorily with bad lay-out or obsolete development,
(iii) to provide for the relocation of population or industry or the replacement of open-space in the course of the development or redevelopment of any other area,
 (iv) for any other purpose specified in the plan. (4)

The first two reasons were the basis for introducing the legislation in 1944, and were the most commonly used to designate Comprehensive

17

Development Areas (CDA). In that sense they differ from their successors in the new legislation, namely the Action Areas. There are other substantial differences as well: the relationship between the whole of the local authority's planning area and that of the CDA was not clearly established, nor was the period of development necessarily limited. The procedures followed for the CDA were different and more cumbersome than those now established for local plans. (5) However, leaving aside changes in the way a local area would be treated now as compared with 30 years ago, the plans for a CDA would be very similar to certain local plans, in particular Action Area plans. The legislation specifically mentions the similarities between the two when dealing with land acquisition and compensation. So Schedule 23 of the Town & Country Planning Act 1971 stated:

'In the Land Compensation Act 1961 any reference to an area defined in the current development plan as an area of comprehensive development shall be construed as a reference to an action area for which a local plan is in force.' (6)

An example of how the two types of plan can converge is provided by Covent Garden, an area originally designated as a CDA and confirmed as such by the Secretary of State. It is now the subject of a local plan as an Action Area of the Greater London Development Plan. (7)

### Town-centre maps and other plans

Local authorities prepared these non-statutory plans when they wanted to promote the renewal of the central area of a town. They were intended to show the background to the policies for the town centre, relating them to the rest of the town or region, and in many cases to attract private investment to the area. The similarities with present-day local plans went further in that they were expected to be a guide for coordinating private and public development. (8)

Other 'inset' maps for any particular area of a county, for which a local authority wanted to plan in detail, could be prepared. Most of them were non-statutory, often known as 'bottom-drawer maps', and they were prepared in very diverse circumstances and for a variety of purposes. Again leaving aside changes in planning philosophy, many of them were in spirit, if not always in form, very similar to the present local plans. In fact the Department of the Environment's Memorandum on Structure and Local Plans of July 19 1977 specifically stated in para 4.4:

'In areas which are covered by an operative structure plan, existing informal plans which are not inconsistent with the structure plan should be regarded as draft local plans. . .' (9)

Other plans can be prepared for specific areas such as: conservation areas, general improvement areas, environmental areas, shopping centres, industrial areas, housing development areas, etc.

For all these types of areas, detailed plans were and still are prepared

18

with the idea that substantial change is to occur within a more or less defined period of time. Not all of these plans can or need be statutorily enforceable and some do not come under town-planning legislation. They are generally not comprehensive, ie they deal mainly with some particular aspect of an area, which is perceived by the local authority as the main issue. In the future most of these plans could be incorporated in local plans and therefore become statutorily enforceable. We will come back to them in later chapters.

Before going into details of the legislation, it can be concluded that the main innovation of the 1968 Town & Country Planning Act in relation to local plans is to have made them a part of the statutory planning process and to have given them a specific role and a relationship to the rest of the planning machinery.


### The PAG report and the 1968 legislation

In 1964, the Ministry of Housing and Local Government set up the Planning Advisory Group (PAG) to review the future of the development plans system. They reported in 1965—The Future of Development Plans—and the following are some of their main conclusions. (10)

The 1947 Town & Country Planning Act and its later amendments had created a comprehensive planning system which covered the whole country, had laid the basis for the exercise of development control, given the public confidence in the exercise of planning controls, and provided a machinery for public objections to the plans. On the negative side, the development plans prepared by the local planning authorities were very detailed, in terms of zoning for example, but could not guarantee that the suggested pattern of development would ever take effect. They gave a false appearance of certainty and stability, and after a while became too rigid. A cumbersome machinery for their preparation and approval meant that out-of-date plans could not be reviewed fast enough. Additionally, this overloaded state of the planning machinery led to numerous planning appeals which took a long time to be decided upon and added even more to the work of the Ministry. In other aspects, development plans were not detailed enough and did not give an indication of what a particular area would really be like if the proposed plan was implemented. Finally, a lack of coordination between authorities meant no development of regional policies, and the planning process did not allow for any significant form of public participation. (11)

The PAG report suggested, therefore, a new system of development plans which would be divided into two parts, and, with some modification, this was adopted by the 1968 Town & Country Planning Act and consolidated in the 1971 Act. In the future, development plans would consist of two parts:

19

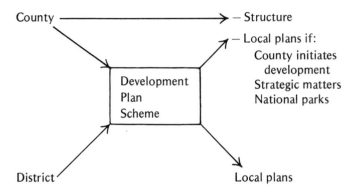

**Fig. 1: Development plan scheme (Local Government Act 1972).**

I   The *structure plan* is a general policy-document for large areas (generally counties) translating national and regional, economic and social policies into the local planning authority's area context. It will indicate areas where urgent and comprehensive action is needed but without fixing definite boundaries to them; these are the Action Areas and they will be the subject of local plans (see below). Structure plans are to be submitted to the Secretary of State for approval, and before taking a decision he shall ensure that the public has had a chance to express its views and discuss the merits and faults of the plan's proposals.

II   The more detailed *local plans* are to interpret and apply the proposals of the structure plan, to serve as a guide to developers, and as a medium to coordinate public and private action. They should enable interested parties to appreciate and comment on specific proposals. In general cases, local plans would not need ministerial approval; however, proposals in local plans have to fit within the general policies of the structure plan and take into account proposals of neighbouring areas and representations from the public. (12)

*Types of local plans*
Regulation 15 of the Town & Country Planning (Structure and Local Plans) Regulations 1974 established three types of local plans:

*District plans* for the comprehensive planning of large areas over a relatively long period of time. They can (but need not) cover the whole administrative area of a district planning-authority. They are to provide a link between the broad strategy of the structure plans and more specific proposals.

*Action Area plans* have already been mentioned. They are for the comprehensive planning of fairly restricted areas where change is to occur
20

over the next ten years or so. These are probably the most characteristic of the local plans. They are to deal with development, redevelopment or improvement and should be prepared for areas that have been indicated in the structure plan. They should provide a framework in which private and public developers would work in a coordinated way but with freedom.

*Subject plans* to deal with special issues in detail. These issues may cover a wide area and not only a specific district, and they need not be area-based. The DOE's Circular 55/77, Memorandum on Structure and Local Plans specified the circumstances in which a subject plan would be appropriate:

'(a) the subject has such limited interactions with other planning matters, nor the subject itself, will suffer if the subject is planned in isolation; and

(b) either: (i) there is a need to develop local policies and proposals in advance of comprehensive plans; or (ii) other matters in that area are of insufficient importance to justify planning comprehensively.' (13)

Examples are land-reclamation or a policy towards a network of footpaths. Main topics such as housing, employment etc should generally be part of the structure plans and not subject plans. On the other hand, there may be arguments in favour of considering the 'design guidelines' (see page 109 published by various authorities as subject plans.

## Form and function of local plans

Since there will exist a wide variety of local plans, the legislation is deliberately general with regard to the presentation of local plans, and has mainly established general principles. The development plans' manual stated the four main functions of local plans as being:

1  Applying the strategy of the structure plan: local plans have to develop and apply its policies, showing proposed changes in development and use of land.

2  Providing a detailed basis for development control: local plans will eventually replace the present development plans (existing under the 1962 legislation) as documents for development control, and they should give precise information of sites allocated for specific uses, defining policies, standards, etc.

3  Providing a basis for coordinating development: one of the main purposes of the new system is to go beyond the restrictive character of development control by achieving a close coordination of public and private investment.

4  Bringing local and detailed planning issues before the public: this goes well beyond the discussion of general issues that takes place at structure plan level. The plan's detailed effect on the area is presented to the public, showing in particular how it will affect people's interests. (14)

The presentation of local plans will include a 'proposals map' on an Ordnance Survey base, showing existing land-uses and firm proposals for

21

change, plus areas where special development-control policies will apply. Whenever needed, additional illustrative material will be added to clarify specific points. A written statement will give the background to the plan and the reasoning behind it, and will indicate the order in which inter-dependent proposals should be carried out. The Regulations indicate that it should include the following items: a description of the area, its problems, characteristics, etc; a summary of the structure plans' policies affecting the area; a description of relationships between the area and surrounding ones; an explanation of policies and proposals in the plan; an indication of the intended phasing and relationship between proposals; a description of the means of implementation, eg finance and agencies involved. (15)

Later chapters will discuss how well the planning system is coping with the above requirements, and at this stage it is sufficient to say that the reality is not always in line with the legislative theory.

*Preparation of local plans*
Local planning authorities may start preparing local plans at any time: they do not have to wait for the approval of the corresponding structure plan, although they cannot adopt the local plan until the structure plan has had ministerial approval. If it has been approved and it indicates Action Areas, the local authority shall start preparing Action Area plans as soon as possible. The Secretary of State has the power to direct a local authority to prepare a local plan for a particular area at any time. (16)

As mentioned before, the proposals in a local plan have to conform to those of the structure plan and be consistent with those of other local plans. Different local plans can be prepared for different purposes for the same part of any area, but not two similar local plans; for example, a district plan, an Action Area plan and a subject plan can overlap, but two district plans cannot. (17)

The regulations relating to structure and local plans were first produced before the 1974 reform of local government, when it was assumed that if a two-tier system emerged, the top tier (counties) would be responsible for structure plans and the lower tier (districts) for local plans. Some difficulties could be foreseen insofar as, although districts were authorised to start preparing local plans at any time, they would not have the necessary framework until the structure plan was completed. On the other hand, a district authority might see the overall priorities from a different point of view than that of its neighbours, and substantial conflicts could ensue when various districts would be competing for scarce resources within a county.

The Local Government Act 1972 tried to clarify the situation by allocating responsibilities. It introduced the Development Plan Scheme (Section 183, now inserted as Section 10C of the 1971 Town & Country
22

Planning Act). The county planning authority, in consultation with the district planning authorities, would designate the local planning authority, whether county or district, responsible for the preparation of the local plans, specifying the title and nature of the plans, setting out a programme for their preparation and the relationships between various local plans. In preparing the Development Plan Scheme, staff resources and the areas which most urgently need a local plan should be given particular consideration. The Act establishes a general presumption in favour of district authorities undertaking local plans, except in national parks. However, in certain cases, if the issues are considered to be of strategic importance (eg when major highway interests are involved), or if a large part of the development is to be initiated by the county council, the latter is to be responsible for the local plan. The Development Plan Scheme is not subject to approval by the Secretary of State, but, in cases of conflict between authorities, it may be necessary for him to intervene and prepare the scheme. The Development Plan Scheme does not apply to London, where the boroughs are responsible for local plans except in the case of certain Action Areas identified in the GLDP. (18)

*Approval of local plans*
Assuming the structure plan has had ministerial approval, procedures for the adoption of the local plans can start. Copies of it have to be put forward for inspection by the public and a copy sent to the Secretary of State. A period of time, no less than six weeks, is to be set for people to make objections and representations. A statement has to be sent to the Secretary of State indicating what steps have been taken to hear the public's views and to take them into account. (19) In January 1977 the Waterloo District Plan prepared by the London Borough of Lambeth was sent back by the DOE because the local authority had not fulfilled the statutory requirements for public participation.

Since the Local Government Act 1972, local plans prepared by district authorities (this does not apply to London) have to obtain a certificate from the county council establishing their conformity with the structure plan before they can be put on deposit. (20) If there are relevant objections to the plan, a public inquiry is to be called, and this will be headed by a person appointed by the DOE but called and paid by the local authority. The report on the inquiry is to go to the authority and not to the Secretary of State. Providing objections have been dealt with and the recommendations of the inspector taken into account, the local authority, county or district as the case may be, can approve and adopt the plan. A major innovation is therefore the fact that, in normal circumstances, the Secretary of State will not be involved in the approval of local plans. However, if he considers that any of the provisos made above have not been taken into account, or in other exceptional circumstances, he may call in the local plan for his own approval. (21)

### Allocation of responsibilities
From this brief outline of the legislative framework, it appears that since the 1972 Local Government Act, the county authorities have become the masters of the planning system. Districts can make representations if they are not satisfied with the development plan scheme—and indeed they should be consulted during its preparation—but the initiative lies in the hands of the first-tier authority, whicn can prepare local plans itself, if it so decides, on the basis that the issues considered are of strategic character.

Up to now, most of the county authorities have been busy preparing their structure plans, and this has consumed most of their resources. On the other hand, the districts, often starved of staff resources, have been mainly committed to daily matters such as development control and trying to become acquainted with the recently created areas and their issues of concern. Therefore, on the one hand there is a powerful authority taking strategic decisions but not being able or willing to involve itself with small detail, and consequently often missing the important points that people are concerned with and, on the other hand, weaker authorities, at best aware of local issues, which are incapable of providing the context in which action should be taken. The result has often been planning by default, reaction too late to real problems, a general frustration with the whole planning system, and in some cases the replacing of the statutory process by some other forms of policy-making under varying titles which avoid the planning legislation and related requirements on participation and approval.

Two cases in point were discussed at a meeting of the Town Planning Forum at the Town & Country Planning Association in November 1974, one from London, the other from South Hampshire; both seem fairly typical of the state of affairs at the time throughout the country. (22)

In South Hampshire, the county had indicated a number of local plans which it intended to deal with itself. A number of districts—Southampton and Portsmouth as major cities excepted—were starved of staff, and although they had identified problems that needed attention in terms of local planning, they did not have the strength to demand higher priority in the county's allocation of resources. They therefore intended to prepare 'unofficial' plans or policy papers, in between dealing with daily matters and canvassing the opinions of parish councils and local organisations.

In London, the situation was (and is) even more confusing. The Greater London Development Plan, finally approved, is itself the structure plan, and there is nothing between it and the borough's local plans. The
24

borough councils were therefore expected to prepare borough-wide district plans. The Secretary of State sent an advice-note to London's chief planning officers in April 1974 stating:

'It is not intended that the regulations governing the making of local plans in London shall require either a single district plan to be prepared for the whole borough, or that all of the borough shall necessarily be covered by district plans. It is anticipated nevertheless that London boroughs will wish to prepare such all-inclusive plans and this note is written with this end in mind.' (23)

The boroughs soon discovered that these borough-wide plans were much too general and covered an area too wide to be seen as local by the people affected. Furthermore, they would take so long to prepare that some authorities divided their area and started preparing smaller district plans, which would either be published separately or have no official status until added together to form the statutory borough plan. As a substitute to statutory local plans, a number of boroughs produced a 'community plan' as the real policy-making instrument. Camden Borough Council managed to produce a borough plan in record time and was the first London borough to do so. However, though called a local plan, it has all the characteristics of a structure plan, including a key diagram.

The conflicts arising from the allocation of responsibilities encompass a number of local government services, but seem to be exacerbated at the planning level. In August 1976, the Chairman of Barnsley Development and Planning Committee was quoted as saying: 'The county are trying to rob us of functions which are strictly for district councils. It is in effect a takeover bid. They are trying to delocalise local government.' (24) And in April 1976, David Beardmore of Avon Planning Department, stated: 'Such goodwill and cooperation are not apparent in many county/ district relationships and it is this area, more than any other, that has given rise to the most friction and the greatest number of disputes in the ad-ministration of development control since April 1974.' (25)

This state of affairs can only bring planning into worst disrepute, and it is hoped that as the system matures, the allocation of responsibilities will be made clearer. People are confused by the number of different plans discussed and the various authorities involved: they wonder what the planners are doing, why decisions take so long, and why are they not consulted when they are taken. If community plans manage to integrate the local government machinery into a real corporate system, they should be more than welcome, but local plans should be the means to achieve integration on the smaller scale. Town-planning should not be left outside community planning on grounds of being too cumbersome, too hot to handle, or irrelevant. In particular, following the community land legisla-tion of 1970, local authorities will need to have a document on which to base their requirements for acquisition. (26)

What then are the measures which could be taken to improve the present system? To start with, it would seem that the system should pause and look back to its original objectives, which were to simplify the whole planning machinery and make it more flexible and accessible to the public. The counties are too large to achieve this easily, and therefore responsibility for preparing local plans should clearly lie with the districts. This in turn means that they must be given the powers and the resources to assume this responsibility. If necessary, they should get assistance from the counties, for instance through staff secondment (as a number of counties are already doing). Any district or borough which sees the need for a local plan, whether district, Action Area or subject plan, should be able to embark upon it without having to wait for a structure plan, a development plan scheme or for a county council's initiative.

With regard to the approval of the plans, the sequence imposed by the legislation is perhaps the logical one, and, understandably, it tried to avoid a situation where proposals made at higher level could be negated or pre-empted by those at the lower level. However, some way needs to be found to speed action at local level within the general framework, and this would be achieved if local plans could be approved, at least provisionally, before the structure plans. If total disagreement occurred between the two-tier authorities, it is doubtful whether the structure plan could be easily approved or implemented; if there is agreement, there is no reason to wait; and if, subsequently, overall policies demand the modification of local proposals, the plan could be amended accordingly. The Secretary of State could always, as he can at the moment, take the ultimate decision in cases of conflict. This right of appeal to the Ministry should however be used sparingly, or the system may become as overloaded as it was under the pre-1968 legislation, because the Ministry became too involved in matters of detail. (27)

Interestingly, the government is aware of the problems created by the structure/local plans relationship, at least insofar as its employment policies are concerned. In Circular 71/77, Local Government and The Industrial Strategy, it is stated that, pending approval of structure plans, 'a draft local plan would be a material consideration in the exercise of development control'. (28) Similarly in the case of London, the government, realising the need to allow some local initiative and independence, has omitted the certification of local plans by the GLC from the procedures for adoption. However, as a safeguard which seems much more rational than certification, the GLC can appear as an objector at the public enquiry. (29)

To conclude this general introduction, it must be stressed that local plans were brought into British legislation to make the planning system simpler and more sensitive to people's demands, and that, as far as can be judged at the moment, the attempt may be in danger of failure. To be successful, suggested measures demand a better level of understanding and collaboration between authorities than obtains in the present climate, where distrust and competition seem all too common. David Beardmore provides an appropriate ending to this chapter:

'It is apparent that the reasonably smooth working of the development control process since April 1974 has occured in spite of rather than due to the Local Government Act 1972, and the resultant two-tier system. . . Where the political control of the county authority differs from that in any large district within it, the potential for inter-authority friction is at its greatest.' (30)

## REFERENCES

1  For a wider discussion of pre-war legislation, see for instance J B Cullingworth, *Town & country planning in Britain* George Allen & Unwin, London, 1974, chapter 1.

2  Town & Country Planning Act 1947, c51, HMSO, London.

3  Town & Country Planning Act 1944, c47, HMSO, London.

4  Town & Country Planning Act 1947, Part 2, S5(3), HMSO, London.

5  For further discussion of CDA procedures, see J B Cullingworth, op cit, pp78-80 and 255-260.

6  Town & Country Planning Act 1971, c78, HMSO, London, Part 1, Schedule 23, referring to the Land Compensation Act 1961, c33.

7  The Greater London Council (Covent Garden) GLC Action Area Plan adopted January 24 1978, published by the Greater London Council, May 1978, Section A, Introduction, p9.

8  Ministry of Housing and Local Government, 'Town centres: approach to renewal' *Planning bulletin* no 1, HMSO, London, 1962.

9  Department of the Environment, The Town & Country Planning Act 1971: Memorandum on Structure and Local Plans, Circular 55/77, 'Existing informal plans' paras 4.4 and 4.5, p44.

10  MOHLG, *The future of development plans* Report of the Planning Advisory Group, HMSO, London 1965.

11  MOHLG 1965 op cit, paras 1.6 to 1.32 for a review of the state of the planning system in 1964.

12  Town & Country Planning Act 1971, c78, HMSO, London, Part 2. See also MOHLG, *Development plans: a manual of form and content* HMSO, London, 1970.

13  DOE, Town & Country Planning (Structure and Local Plans) Regulations 1974, S15. See also the above mentioned Development Plans Manual, Section 7.2 and Circular 55/77, paras 3.6 to 3.10.

14  MOHLG, *Development plans: manual of form and content* paras 7.3 and 7.4 and Circular 55/77 para 3.1, p27.

15  DOE, Town & Country Planning (Structure and Local Plans) Regulations 1974, Section 17 and Schedule 2 part 2.

16  Town & Country Planning Act 1971, S11, as modified by Local Government Act 1972, Schedule 16.

17  Town & Country Planning Act 1971, S11(4) and Circular 55/77, S3.10.

18  For the development plan scheme, see Circular 55/77, S3.11-3.23. This circular does not apply to London (para 1.6) where the Town & Country Planning (Local Plans for Greater London) Regulations 1974 do apply.

19  Town & Country Planning Act 1971, S12-14 as amended by Local Government Act 1972, S16. See also Circular 55/77, S3.59-3.78, 'Procedures for Adoption of Local Plans'.

20  Local Government Act 1972, S16.

21  See Note (19). The DOE has also produced a booklet *Local plans: public local inquiries. A guide to procedure* HMSO, 1977 which gives details on inquiries.

22  See report of meeting in *Planning*, Nov 15 1974, 'Local plans: who decides issues'.

23  Interim advice on the making of district plans in London, para 1. This was sent to Mr A Deans, Borough Planning Officer of the London Borough of Greenwich with a covering letter which stated: 'The term "district plan" is used throughout the Note but implicit is that most, if not all boroughs will wish to prepare a single district plan for the whole borough'. This note was circulated to all London Borough planning offices.

24  *Planning*, August 6 1976, 'Councils clash over structure plans'.

25  D Beardmore, 'An uneasy partnership in development control' in *The planner* vol 62, no 3, April 1976, p74.

26  Community Land Act 1975, c77, HMSO, London.

27  The Inspector's report on the inquiry into the objections to the Action Area plan for the Western Wards of Fareham (Hampshire County Council), February 1978 paras 29 and 30, is worth referring to both for its ambiguity and for the doors it leaves open.

28  DOE Circular 71/77, 'Local government and the industrial strategy', July 11 1977, para 9.

29  For London, The Town & Country Planning (Local Plans for Greater London) Regulations 1974 apply. See also Town & Country Planning (Local Planning Authorities in Greater London) Regulations 1978.

30  D Beardmore, op cit, p74.

Chapter 2

# THE ESTABLISHMENT OF THE FRAMEWORK

The following chapters are intended to give a general introduction to the planning process, specifically related to local plans. Of course there is no unique kind of process, but rather a series of individual variations around a main theme, and so a fairly traditional format is presented, emphasising what is special about local plans as opposed to other kinds of planning, and the differences between the theoretical model and the way this is applied in practice are discussed. It must be stressed that existing experience with regard to local plans within the present legislation is very limited; and some of the stages may be fairly controversial—those aspects relating to public participation, for example. However, a number of plans published, sometimes only in draft form, have been analysed to provide the examples that illustrate the process. (1)

Table 1 and figure 2 show an outline of the process based on a comprehensive rationality model and on the satisfaction of objectives. Each part will be developed in turn, although some stages may be grouped together, and it will be evident in following the process that not all authorities adopt this method. For example, Chichester District Council opted for a 'strategic choice' method of solving a series of identified problems for their Manhood local plan. (2) However, practical examples of divergence from the basic model do not negate the latter's general validity.

If the plan was for a small, isolated island, with no ties with the outside world, this part of the process might not be needed; there would be no external pressures or influences to be borne in mind, and the effects of planning for the island would have little repercussion on other localities. However, in real situations, the local area is part of a larger system, be it the city, the county, the region or the country. It is hardly necessary to emphasise here the interrelationships which exist between the various aspects of society. B McLoughlin has done so very adequately, as have other authors of the 'systems approach' school (3); as John Friedmann said in 1966, 'It is satisfying to think of everything being related to everything else'. (4) It is sufficient to repeat here that activities developed within the local area being considered will have linkages with other activities outside it; the inhabitants of the area are not likely to limit their lives to the area's boundaries, nor is the area likely to be closed to outsiders.

1  THE ESTABLISHMENT OF THE FRAMEWORK
   (a)  National, regional and structure plan context
   (b)  Infrastructure
   (c)  Relationship with adjacent areas
   (d)  Role of the area
   (e)  Definition of the area

2  INITIAL STAGES OF PUBLIC PARTICIPATION

3  INITIAL DEFINITION OF GOALS

4  ANALYSIS OF THE LOCAL SITUATION
   (a)  Physical characteristics
   (b)  Social structure
   (c)  Economic structure
   (d)  Opportunities and constraints: factors contributing to and
        inhibiting change

5  REDEFINITION OF PROBLEM

6  SECOND STAGE OF PUBLIC PARTICIPATION: REPORT OF SURVEY

7  GENERATION OF ALTERNATIVE STRATEGIES
   (a)  Objectives
   (b)  Policies
   (c)  Design and development control policies
   (d)  Financial resources/cost
   (e)  Developers' contribution/local authorities' contribution

8  EVALUATION—THIRD STAGE OF PUBLIC PARTICIPATION

9  CHOICE OF BEST ALTERNATIVES
   (a)  Consultation with public and developers
   (b)  Public inquiry
   (c)  Adoption

10  IMPLEMENTATION
   (a)  Reconsideration of structure plan policies
   (b)  Local authorities development
   (c)  Development control

11  MONITORING


**Table 1: The local planning process**

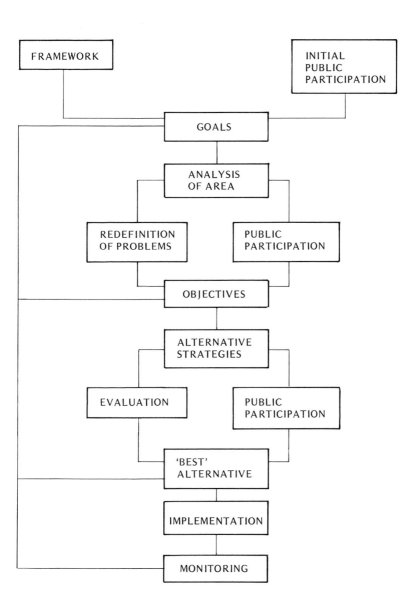

Fig 2: The local planning process.

The first step in the process is, therefore, crucial: the area for which the plan is to be prepared has to be placed in its context.

*National, regional and county context*
If the corresponding structure plan has been approved, it will provide the basic framework for the local plans. The *Development plans manual* and DOE Circular 55/77 cite the following amongst the functions of structure plans:

   i   Interpreting national and regional policies in terms appropriate to the areas.

   ii   Providing a framework for local plans.

   iii   Indicating action areas and explaining the nature of the intended treatment.

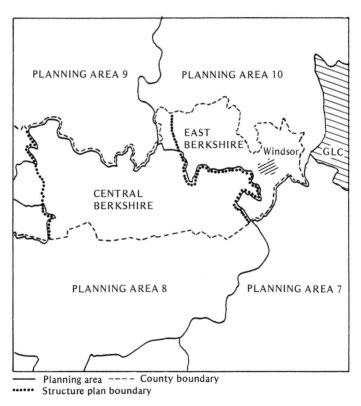

——— Planning area   – – – County boundary
•••••• Structure plan boundary

Fig 3: An area in its context: Windsor Town Centre. Source: Berkshire C. C. and the Royal Borough of Windsor and Maidenhead, Windsor Town Centre District Plan.

In relation to local plans, the manual states as their first function:

To apply the strategy of the structure plan: they will develop the policies and general proposals in it. (5)

If, however, there is no approved structure plan to turn to for the framework, or if it does not provide sufficient information, it will be necessary to search elsewhere.

Regional and national policies may be of a varied nature, more or less precise, and affecting the area more or less directly. For instance, at national level there may be an employment policy tending to detract industrial investment from the region in which the area considered is located. On the other hand, within the regional context, the area may have been earmarked as a growth area. Similarly, there may be national housing policies encouraging housing development in the area (through, say, the availability of grants or Exchequer subsidies). At another level, the area may be affected by such constraints as 'green belt' policies. (6)

The state of progress of the structure plan has, of course, to be considered, since it may indicate the way national and regional policies are to be interpreted. Furthermore, it is likely that there will already be policies, officially or unofficially approved, which affect the locality. The South Oxofrdshire District Council, in their district plan for Wallingford, quote the Strategic Plan for the South East, the existing Consultative Document on the Oxfordshire County Structure Plan and the DOE's decision on an appeal against refusal of planning permission for residential development in the area, in order to establish that Wallingford is not to be a growth area. (7)

The local area will have to be served by utilities (drainage, water supply, electricity, etc) which are part of wider networks not controlled by the local planning authority. These may be capable of taking an increased load, or they may already be working to full capacity. In the latter case, there may be plans for expansion of the networks for some years ahead. Possibilities of development in the local area will depend on the state of these networks. The South Hampshire Structure Plan, for instance, stated:

'As a result of the past scale of growth in the area, much of the drainage system has reached its physical capacity. Unlike transportation, this problem has imposed an absolute limitation to further development in particular areas. . .' (8)

Similarly, the road and transportation networks have to be analysed, and the relationship between the local area and the existing and proposed networks. There are cases when changes in the road system provoke the need to prepare a local plan: the building of a by-pass or a motorway, or change of the whole traffic pattern in an urban area to relieve congestion. In other cases, although transport issues may not be the generators of the local plan, they will still have an important influence on the area. In Wallingford, for instance, traffic is a problem but the district council has to acknowledge the priorities set by the county council and, therefore, quotes the latter as highway authority:

'Because of the procedures which have to be followed, the earliest practical date that construction could start on a by-pass, even with a decision now on which scheme should proceed, is 1980.' (9)

Decisions at local level depend not only upon related decisions at a higher level, but also upon those at the same level in other areas. The local area considered must, therefore, be related to others in the same county or region, and the relationship may not always be an easy one. Conflicts can occur because priority levels may be differently perceived by the authority directly concerned and the neighbouring ones. In principle, the development plan scheme should solve this kind of problem by setting up a programme for local plans. However, conflicts may still occur—for instance, over the levels of investment.

Within one district authority itself, priorities have to be set to ensure that local plans are prepared for the areas most in need of them. Barnsley District Council gives an interesting example in this respect. They chose fifty indicators to classify priority needs at ward level, including all available information from local authority sources; not only on housing, but also on statistics from the area health authority and the probation service. (10) Coventry, on the other hand, already had a sophisticated management system, coordinating activities on a city-wide basis according to priorities: an Action Area programme could be set up by considering intensive changes under various topic headings, and relating them to each other. This city was privileged in that, by pioneering the new planning system, it avoided at the time the constraints of the new local government structure. (11) More or less similar methods have been developed by other authorities and then used to discuss priorities with the counties in preparing the development planning schemes. In more fortunate areas, various authorities managed to agree; and J Griffiths, from the Hertfordshire County Planning Department, could say in August 1976: 'The concept has developed of "planning for Hertfordshire" and not "county planning and district planning in Hertfordshire"'. (12)

Friction between areas may also arise because of the lack of information about the intentions of a neighbouring authority. For example, the provision by district council A of certain facilities, say a secondary school or a shopping centre, may attract people or investors, and detract them from adjacent district B. It might, therefore, be unwise for district council B to build similar facilities. However, district council A may not want their intentions to be known until their plans are well under way; B, meanwhile, may advance in the same direction. Eventually, one of the authorities finds that it has undertaken a substantial amount of abortive work. With the emphasis on public participation, and the supervision of local planning by county authorities, this kind of conflict may occur less

34

frequently, but it highlights the importance of sharing information between neighbouring authorities right from the beginning of the planning process.

*Role of the area*
Having placed the study area within its wider context, it should be possible then to establish whether or not the area has a special role within that context. In very exceptional cases, a local area is totally inward-looking, and changes in it have little effect outside its boundaries. In other extreme cases, the area has a very specific role to play, which has been defined at the outset, and may be the reason for a local plan—such as a regional shopping centre, a dormitory housing development in the commuter belt, or an industrial park. In most cases, the area's role may exist, but may not be easy to define. Windsor town centre is an example where the importance of the role was acknowledged by the planners from the beginning of the process, particularly in relation to two neighbouring towns, Slough and Maidenhead:

'The proximity of these towns, allied to their different strengths and weaknesses, creates a well-knit group, each settlement contributing to the others. Therein lies the danger of planning for one town without due regard to the future plans of its neighbours.' (13) Covent Garden in London is an example of the kind of area for which there is a multiplicity of expected roles: a central-area role, a tourist attraction, an entertainment centre; it is supposed to help in solving the housing shortage of inner London and it has its own indigenous problems as well. Additionally, it may be called to play other more specific roles (eg a mooted world centre for stamp trading). Another area with similar characteristics, in terms of the role or roles it is meant to play, is London's Dockland. (14)

*Boundaries of the local area*
Up to now a local area has been mentioned without its boundaries being defined. It is interesting to note that in a majority of published local plans, this point is not even mentioned, as if the area boundaries were obvious. It is only in exceptional cases that they are delineated, although sometimes they are defined as part of the planning brief. In most cases, however, the planning team will have been given a location with only approximate boundaries. These can be determined at the beginning of the process or, as suggested here, after the framework has been considered. In any case, lines on maps should be treated with care, and accepted as flexible and temporary, since revisions of the boundaries may be necessary at later stages. These lines are important in that they define a selective resource allocation: a building or a plot of land within the lines will be treated differently from one outside them.

35

# Covent Garden

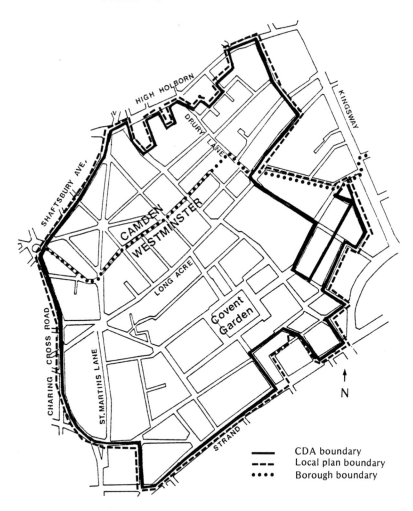

Fig 4: Boundaries of a local plan with no obvious physical definition. Source: Greater London Council, Covent Garden GLC Action Area Plan.

In the case of Action Areas, the legislation is specific in determining that structure plans indicate boundaries; but only when the local plan is being prepared will the exact boundaries be defined. (15) In the case of district plans, these need not cover the whole administrative area of a district authority, and there may well be several district plans covering one area. In the case of the London boroughs, the Department of the Environment indicated (April 1974) that it would like them to produce one district plan for the whole borough; but in practice, a number of authorities have subdivided their area into smaller districts with the intention of amalgamating the plans into one document at a later date. Subject plans are not necessarily area-based and, therefore, would extend to the boundaries of the subject treated, within the administrative area.

How then are the boundaries to be fixed? How is the area to be defined? In some cases, the area may have a geographical unity and its boundaries can be easily established by physical features such as a river, a railway embankment, a motorway. The Coventry canal is one of the boundaries of the Eden Street area, and the Thames bounds the Richmond town centre plan. (16) In other cases it will be more difficult to define perimeters and various approaches can be tried. These must differ from the methods suggested by various authors to define larger areas: the extent of a system of transportation, the radius of coverage of a local newspaper, the dependence on financial institutions, the dependence of borderline services on various other services, etc. All of them may sometimes work in the case of districts, but are unlikely to be of any use for defining the boundaries of an Action Area. Some form of unity, which gives the area its identity, must be found. The following are some of the more frequent types of unity that may be perceived.

*Unity of physical characteristics*: an area that has common physical features throughout can be taken as the study area—for example, a type of buildings (eg nineteenth century terraced housing); a type of land-use (industrial area or shopping centre); a natural characteristic (an area prone to flooding). The unity may also be provided by a combination of these. One of the few plans that mentions the problem of boundaries, the Windsor town centre plan, states: 'The definition of this boundary was based on the fairly precise division between the predominantly commercial area of activity and the adjoining inner residential area'. (17)

*Unity of social characteristics*: these may not always be easy to perceive at this stage, but a survey may reveal that an area's residents have some common characteristic which identifies them within the context of a wider area. The obvious example is a ghetto inhabited by an ethnic minority, but there are other situations where a neighbourhood is perceived as such according to its inhabitants.

*Unity of problems*: an area may be defined by the geographical extension of a certain problem or a combination of problems. These can be of various kinds: housing overcrowding and multi-occupation; traffic congestion; derelict buildings; the disappearance of a major employment generator, etc. The existence of a specific problem may have triggered the need for a local plan. However, it often happens that the problems have an over-spill effect on adjacent areas, which might thus have to be included in the local plan area as well.

*Unity of ownership*: the fact that an area is in one ownership, private or public, has sometimes been considered as the basis for defining a plan's area. Although this may be practical in certain cases, it does not necessarily correspond to a real unity and may not always be a good guide for defining an area. However, like administrative boundaries, it can be useful for purely pragmatic reasons.

The City of Coventry's plan for the Eagle Street Action Area provides a good example of boundaries defined by a variety of factors:

'The total area of the Action Area is 73.6 acres and falls into three main categories:

Property within the Comprehensive Development Area, as defined in the 1972 Review Town Map.

Property within the George Eliot Road General Improvement Area.

Adjacent property, not included in the above, but which has clear physical and social links with these areas. . .

The Action Area is also often known by residents as ' "Five Ways".' (18)

At the end of this first part of the local planning process, the planning team should have a knowledge of the background of the area considered, and should have determined the context in which it is being planned. Some of the most important aspects of local planning have been touched upon, but before developing them further, the question arises of 'how local is local? '

A comment on this particular question comes from the DOE Note 1/78 on local plans which reflects present concern on certain subjects beyond legislative requirements. Priorities in the preparation of local plans, to be settled in the development plan scheme, should have regard to such issues as the industrial content of an area, inner city problems, pressure for development, growth areas, etc. (19) When trying to set the area in its context, the planner has to consider national and regional policies as they affect the area; but how far should this go? Should he consider say, the problems of the balance of payments or the effects of the energy crisis on the area? (The answer to the latter may be yes if the area is near the Scottish coast, where oil is being extracted, or in a similar situation.) Should the planner find out what happens in all local areas in the whole of the region, or just those immediately adjacent to the area considered? When trying to define the boundaries for the area, should he limit himself
38

to one characteristic or one set of problems, or should he go beyond and include those neighbouring areas where local action may have an influence, even if this is not overtly perceived at this stage? The already-quoted Windsor town centre plan had its boundary extended after considerations of this kind:

'However, this rather restrictive definition of the town centre meant that a number of areas of land closely related to the town centre and within the outstanding conservation area were excluded from the study area. Hence the study area as shown includes parts of the town which are considered to be extensions and closely related parts of the town centre.' (20)

Should the planners take into account only the boundaries that residents of an area perceive for their locality, or should they take a more 'objective' point of view? Or, for convenience sake, should they include the whole of an administrative area, even though it may be a heterogeneous one? There are no mandatory answers to any of these questions and each situation will have to be judged on its own merits. However, the planner cannot wait to have all the information about, and a perfect definition of, the area before he starts planning for it. The main thing is for him to retain a certain amount of flexibility and be ready to alter the boundaries and/or investigate further the outer environment.

The involvement of the public and greater knowledge of the area as the planning process develops will help gradually to define it more clearly. In a General Improvement Area in Leicester, two years after the beginning of the planning process, the residents of a street block outside the designated area asked to be included in it; and later on, another group of residents of a different block asked to be taken out of it. At least in theory, and if political interests do not prevent it, it will be possible to change the boundaries when the area has been analysed in more detail. This analysis is the subject of the next chapter. (21)

## REFERENCES

1 For a discussion on various approaches, see R Thompson, 'Camden's local plan: a district-wide approach' in *The planner*, vol 63, no 5, Sept 1977, p145. For a more general description of the process of planning, see J B McLoughlin, *Urban and regional planning*, Faber, London, 1969.

2 Chichester District Council, Manhood Local Plan, Alternatives Report, Feb 1976.

3 J B McLoughlin, op cit.

4 J Friedmann, 'Planning as innovation: the Chilean case', in the *Journal of the American Institute of Planners*, July 1966, p195.

5   Ministry of Housing and Local Government, *Development plans, a manual of form and content*, HMSO, London, 1970; chapter 3, para 3.10, p19 and chapter 7, para 7.3, p40.

6   There is at present another example of conflicting national and subregional policies; the inner areas of London are in the South-East and, therefore, in areas from which national policies would tend to detract industry; but inner area policies for London are now trying to maintain and, if possible increase, industrial employment.

7   South Oxfordshire District Council, District Plan for Wallingford, Draft Local Plan, Jan 1976, pp3-6, para 1.4, The Context of the Plan.

8   Hampshire County Council, South Hampshire Structure Plan, Nov 1973, para 4.57, p34.

9   South Oxfordshire District Council, op cit, para 2.24, p12.

10   *Planning* 114 May 9 1975, p3, 'Tackling local plan priorities—Barnsley style'.

11   J Edwards, 'Organisation' in *The planner*, vol 60, no 1, Jan 1974 pp498-500.

12   J Griffiths, 'Experience in a shire county—Hertfordshire', in *The planner* vol 62, no 5, p140, July/Aug 1976.

13   Berkshire County Council and the Royal Borough of Windsor and Maidenhead, Windsor Town Centre District Plan, Aug 1977, p7, para 3.3.3.

14   Consortium of Greater London Council, Westminster City Council and the London Borough of Camden, Covent Garden's Moving, Covent Garden Area Draft Plan, 1968.

15   Town & Country Planning Act 1971, Part 2, S7 (5), HMSO, London and DOE Circular 55/77 paras 2.32-2.33 and 2.38.

16   London Borough of Richmond upon Thames, Richmond Town Centre, Action Area Plan Report, 1976, p9. City of Coventry, Eden Street Action Area Plan, 1975, para 1.1, p1 and fig 1. See also City of Coventry, Eagle Street Action Area, Written Statement 1975, para 1.02, p1.

17   Berkshire C C and Royal Borough of Windsor and Maidenhead, op cit, para 1.4.1, p4.

18   City of Coventry, Eagle Street Action Area, Written Statement para 1.02, p1.

19   DOE, Local Plans Note 1/78, Form and Content of Local Plans, February 1978, para 6.

20   Berkshire C C and Royal Borough of Windsor and Maidenhead, op cit, para 1.4.1, p4.

21   S Howard, 'An illustration of some of the practical difficulties in GIAs', paper presented to the Town & Country Planning Association Conference on Housing in June 1974.

Chapter 3

# ANALYSIS OF THE LOCAL SITUATION

Within the outline of the process shown in table 1 (page 30), analysis comes
after the initial stages of public participation and the establishment of
goals. Although these are treated in the next chapter under a general
heading, it is important to bear in mind that the collection of information
and the analysis of a situation cannot be done in a void. The planner does
not set out upon a survey for its own sake; he must have a purpose in mind
which will indicate what kind of information he needs and at what level
of detail. As B McLoughlin has stated: 'In general, our information must
be a description of the system we seek to control'. (1)

The analysis of the local situation is, apparently, the most straightforward part of the planning process; but this does not mean that it is
simple. The complexity of the exercise will obviously depend on the type
of area considered. All the *relevant* information is to be collected so as to
understand what are the area's characteristics; and the first problem will
often be to discern what is relevant and what is not. The previous parts of
the process should have given some indication of this.

This stage is what would generally constitute the report of survey
of a local plan. It has been suggested that this could be done in two parts:
a first one to ascertain general characteristics, a second, more detailed one
to look at particular features of the area. The list in table 2 indicates the
types of data that have to be analysed; it has been arbitrarily divided into
physical, social and economic characteristics, but it will be apparent that
items are interrelated. It should be noted that this is not necessarily a
comprehensive list, that some items may not be relevant in all cases, and
that at least part of the information could already have been collected
during earlier stages of the process. The list omits the administrative and
political structures of the area, not because they are not relevant—on the
contrary, they are fundamental—but because they are generally given,
and planners are part of them. It is, therefore, impossible to be objective
about them: they have to be understood, assimilated and made the best
use of, but they will not be part of a written document. (2)

Two important factors have to be taken into account whilst doing this
survey and analysis. The first is that they are intended to record a dynamic
situation. Pressures for change and future potential have to be noted, as

well as the present and past states of affairs. One source of information readily available to the local planning authority is the list of planning applications, which can give a good idea of possible changes generated by the market forces over a period of time.

The second factor is that the planner should discover what is specific about the area and avoid generalities which could apply to any other area. He should try to perceive under each heading what is 'good' or 'bad'; in other words, what are the positive aspects of the area and what are its problems. This involves value-judgments, which should be made explicit, and related where possible to the specific group that expresses them, or to an established standard. For example, if an open space deficiency is recorded it should be pointed out whether this is in relation to standards, the observation of patterns of use, or remarks made by the residents. The degree of satisfaction of various groups should be assessed. Very few parts of the analysis will be objective and this is why this stage is not as straightforward as it might appear at first.

### Physical characteristics
Part of the information on the physical characteristics of the area will be readily available within the local planning authority or in other government departments. For instance, the Environmental Health Officer should have data about housing conditions in the area. Other data will have to be collected by undertaking specific surveys. Although it may appear that the appraisal of physical features cannot be other than objective, value-judgments and discernment will have to be used, particularly in relation to the analysis of the building fabric and environmental aspects. Even the selection of factors being considered may be controversial. A planning consultant was hired by a local authority in Wales to prepare plans for a GIA. (3) The team was busy evaluating the condition of buildings and the possibilities for improving the environment when, through discussions with local residents, they found that the locals' first priority was rubbish collection: not a town-planning issue but an environmental one, which affected the area more than anything else.

Table 2 may look like a shopping list, and is intended as an 'aide-mémoire', since items which can be of unexpected importance might be omitted from the analysis. For instance, geological or topographical facts may seem irrelevant in an urban setting; however, Richmond town centre plan can be quoted: 'The outstanding topographical feature of the borough is Richmond Hill which rises to 55.8 m above sea level in Richmond Park. It slopes steeply on the west towards the River Thames and it is this side that provides the famous view from Terrace Walk'. (4)

Similarly, Uckfield district plan states: 'River flooding is a recurring problem at Uckfield, causing severe dislocation in the town centre'. (5) These are two examples of areas, one urban, the other semi-rural, where natural characteristics have an important role in the future of the area.
42

*Physical characteristics*

    geology, topography, climate, soil, etc

    infrastructure: utilities (drainage, water supply, gas, electricity)
        transport network (roads, public transport, etc)

    existing land uses

    building fabric: age, condition, historical/architectural interest

    environmental aspects: townscape, landscape, outstanding features

    services: schools, shops, health and social services, entertainment,
        open spaces, etc

*Social structure*

    population characteristics: age, sex, households, ties and links,
        social mix, sense of community

    housing tenure

    employment: activity rates, female employment, types of jobs,
        journey to work, employment generation or dispersion

    car ownership

    social vitality and status of the area

    pressure for change, internal or external

*Economic structure*

    land ownership and land values

    local authority control

    rateable value and rates

    economic pressure on the area: over and under employment,
        housing scarcity, attraction of the area, non-conforming
        industries, dependence of industries on one another, etc,
        internal and external factors

    developers' interest in the area

**Table 2: Analysis of the local situation**

The environmental aspects are probably the most difficult to evaluate objectively. G Burke in *Townscapes* states: 'We know a good landscape when we see one. . . Do we know a good townscape when we see one?' (6) We will return to this subject in chapter eight. At this point it is sufficient to emphasise the need to spell out what criteria are being used. Reports that mention the 'special character' of an area without explaining what this means are of little use to the public or to officers in charge of implementing a plan. On the other hand, Richmond Townscape Appraisal, in the town centre plan report already cited (maps 17.1 to 17.4) is a good example of what can be done in this respect. (7)

It is not only the environmental aspects that may be controversial or subjective in appraisal. At the public inquiry into the Covent Garden CDA plan in 1971, a heated discussion took place around the definitions of 'bad layout and obsolete development': 'Actual physical condition is only one factor in the definition of areas of obsolescence in Covent

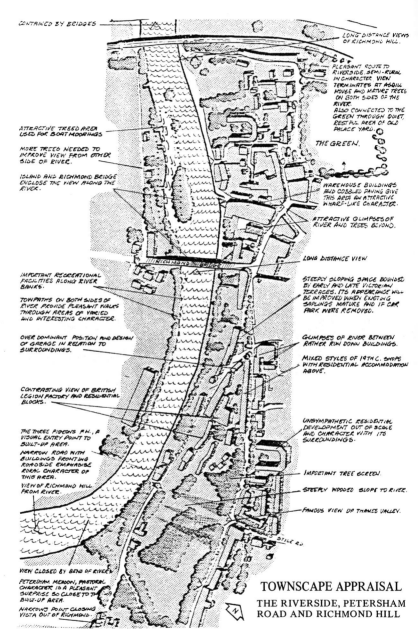

CONTAINED BY BRIDGES

LONG DISTANCE VIEWS OF RICHMOND HILL.

PLEASANT ROUTE TO RIVERSIDE, SEMI-RURAL IN CHARACTER. VIEW TERMINATES AT ASGILL HOUSE AND MATURE TREES ON BOTH SIDES OF THE RIVER.
ALSO CONNECTED TO THE GREEN THROUGH QUIET, RESTFUL AREA OF OLD PALACE YARD.

ATTRACTIVE TREED AREA USED FOR BOAT MOORINGS

THE GREEN.

MORE TREES NEEDED TO IMPROVE VIEW FROM OTHER SIDE OF RIVER.

ISLAND AND RICHMOND BRIDGE ENCLOSE THE VIEW ALONG THE RIVER.

WAREHOUSE BUILDINGS AND COBBLED PAVING GIVE THIS AREA AN ATTRACTIVE WHARF-LIKE CHARACTER.

ATTRACTIVE GLIMPSES OF RIVER AND TREES BEYOND.

LONG DISTANCE VIEW

IMPORTANT RECREATIONAL FACILITIES ALONG RIVER BANKS.

TOWPATHS ON BOTH SIDES OF RIVER PROVIDE PLEASANT WALKS THROUGH AREAS OF VARIED AND INTERESTING CHARACTER.

OVER DOMINANT POSITION AND DESIGN OF GARAGE IN RELATION TO SURROUNDINGS.

STEEPLY SLOPING SPACE BOUNDED BY EARLY AND LATE VICTORIAN TERRACES. ITS APPEARANCE WILL BE IMPROVED WHEN EXISTING SAPLINGS MATURE AND IF CAR PARK WERE REMOVED.

GLIMPSES OF RIVER BETWEEN RATHER RUN DOWN BUILDINGS.

MIXED STYLES OF 19TH C. SHOPS WITH RESIDENTIAL ACCOMMODATION ABOVE.

CONTRASTING VIEW OF BRITISH LEGION FACTORY AND RESIDENTIAL BLOCKS.

UNSYMPATHETIC RESIDENTIAL DEVELOPMENT OUT OF SCALE AND CHARACTER WITH ITS SURROUNDINGS.

THE THREE PIGEONS P.H., A VISUAL ENTRY POINT TO BUILT-UP AREA.

NARROW ROAD WITH BUILDINGS FRONTING ROADSIDE EMPHASISE RURAL CHARACTER OF THIS AREA.

VIEW OF RICHMOND HILL FROM RIVER.

IMPORTANT TREE SCREEN.

STEEPLY WOODED SLOPE TO RIVER.

FAMOUS VIEW UP THAMES VALLEY.

STILE RD.

VIEW CLOSED BY BEND OF RIVER.

PETERSHAM MEADOW, PASTORAL CHARACTER IS A PLEASANT SURPRISE SO CLOSE TO THE BUILT-UP AREA.

NARROW POINT CLOSING VISTA OUT OF RICHMOND.

TOWNSCAPE APPRAISAL
THE RIVERSIDE, PETERSHAM ROAD AND RICHMOND HILL

Fig 5: Analysis of townscape: Richmond Town Centre. Source: London Borough of Richmond upon Thames, Richmond Town Centre, Action Area Plan Report,1976.

44

Garden. Here, due to particular circumstances, the definition of economic obsolescence must rank with that of physical obsolescence in the determination of areas where change should be concentrated.' 'If the building becomes obsolete from its present use point of view, but the fabric of the building is still in reasonable condition, if another use were to be found for it, would it then become obsolete?' (8)

The importance and difficulties of land-use surveys is well documented elsewhere and need not be repeated here: see for instance Jackson and McLoughlin. (9) With regard to housing, there is a vast amount of literature on surveys and evaluation of housing quality. The Ministry of Housing and Local Government and the Department of the Environment have published a number of bulletins on the subject. A fairly comprehensive and well explained text is T L C Duncan's *Measuring housing quality*, which analyses, compares and criticises a number of housing surveys and shows the difficulties of evaluating the quality of housing. (10)

In relation to services, it is particularly important to state what exists, how good or bad it is, and how it satisfies local needs. 'Uckfield does not have any urban parks or general open space other than the small areas found in housing estates. But there is easy access to the surrounding countryside with an extensive network of public footpaths although the river close to the town is not readily accessible. The town is not provided with adequate children's play spaces.' (11) Or, 'Although the higher prices of local goods were acknowledged, the convenience of shops within close proximity to areas of housing appears to offset any discrepancies related to local price ranges.' (12)

In both the above examples, the particular situation of the locality is taken into account, instead of a general planning standard pretending to be of universal application yet too vague to be of any use in a specific case. Neither example gives figures, but both somehow manage to illustrate quite clearly what the issue is.

## Social characteristics

Here the problems of objectivity and reliability of the information are even more complicated. To start with, it is often difficult to find published information for small areas. The Census of Population gives a part of the data needed, but the smallest area for which it is available is an Enumeration District (about 200 households); and its boundaries, or those of a cluster of them, may not coincide with those of the study area. Furthermore, ED boundaries tend to change from one census to the next, making comparisons very difficult. However, the following statement from Richmond town centre plan shows the kind of analysis that can be obtained from the census: 'In 1971 there were about 8,630 economically active persons in the Action Area, and 7,800 were in employment. There was a higher proportion in the non-manual worker socio-economic groups

45

than in the borough as a whole and this proportion had increased since 1966. The total economically active population had decreased, but married women accounted for a higher proportion of it.' (13)

Statistics from most other sources refer to areas far too large to be of any use. Even less reliable would be to use this data for projections into the future. In particular, external pressures such as migrations, employment opportunities elsewhere, regional housing shortages, etc can be very difficult to detect at this scale. Also, the planning proposals themselves will affect the future social structure of the area.

For certain types of area there do exist specialised sources of information: for example, in the case of shopping, the Kelly's directories, the Family Expenditure Survey, the Census of Distribution, accounts and reports of traders or of the Multiple Shop Federation.

It will often be necessary to undertake special surveys and house-to-house interviews. If well designed, these may be very useful, not only in assessing physical, social and economic circumstances, but also in involving and informing the population. But they are time-consuming and they cannot be used for projections. Part of the success of any social survey will depend on good relationships between the planners and the people planned for; and a high level of communication is necessary between them to avoid misunderstandings. When interviewing people, the planner has to interpret the answers and not always take them at face value; but at the same time, he must avoid letting his own prejudices interfere. Herbert Gans has described how suburban households, questioned on their housing attitudes, stated their preference for the suburban type as opposed to inner city; he explained that this was probably less due to the relative location or types of dwellings, than to the fact that in the former case they were owner-occupied and in the latter case tenanted. (14) The kind of information that will be obtained is exemplified by the following quotes from the Eagle Street Action Area social survey: 'Twenty-five per cent have spent more than twenty years in their present dwellings. Thirty per cent had one or more friends in the area. Twenty-five per cent of the working population work shift work or unusual hours. Thirty per cent work either in the Five Ways or in the city centre.' (15) Note that no indication is given of what units are involved—households, people, men, women. Otherwise, the kind of data is appropriate since it would not be available in any published statistic, but is relevant to the planning of the area.

The whole issue of how people perceive their area is still largely undocumented, and often relates mainly to visual aspects. Kevin Lynch has used maps to try to ascertain the 'public image' of a locality, based on certain elements in the environment. Gould and White used similar techniques which they called 'mental maps'. This subject will be expanded in chapter eight. (16) The planner will often have to make his own assumptions, or put forward hypotheses, about the area's vitality and status as

46

perceived by its users, and then test them. Important points are, for example, whether people are proud or ashamed of living in an area, whether they want to move out, whether the facilities provided are used or misused, etc. The planner may be able to refer to secondary sources of information such as the local press, interviews with key persons in the area (such as headmasters, priests, social workers), even graffiti on the walls. By spending a lot of time in the area, he may get the feeling of it; but this is obviously a very subjective method which needs to be carefully controlled.

Finally, the existence of physical features, such as buildings, may be relevant to the social analysis of the area. This is not always the case, but the following example of the Eagle Street Area shows how it can be so: 'The ethnic composition of the area is reflected in the wide range of denominational institutions located in the area which serve not only the local population, but religious groups scattered throughout the city. A number of these institutions play an important part in the lives of immigrant communities in the area for whom religion, for many, is inextricably tied to daily life. The Sikh Temple on Harnall Lane West is a notable example, acting not only as a focal point for religious activities for the Sikh community, but as a social centre which is widely used by this particular group'. (17)

## Economic characteristics
The British system of records makes it difficult to get hold of useful information on economic factors, particularly at a local level. The Census of Population does not include information about income, expenditure or rents. It is possible to get an approximate idea of these either through sample surveys or through alternative records such as the socio-economic groups of the census, which give an indication of incomes, or the housing waiting lists, or the records on rent rebates. These, however, cover a special sample of the population.

It is equally difficult to get information on land ownership. Records are kept by the Land Registry, but this is confidential information not given even to local authorities, except through solicitors engaged in searches for acquisition. The rates records may give some information, and local knowledge, particularly from sources such as local estate agents, can be very useful. Land values, on the other hand, may be fairly easy to assess; but not easy to project into the future, particularly since planning decisions in themselves will affect them.

Specific surveys will always yield information; the already-quoted Eagle Street social survey for example found that: 'Three-quarters of the known net incomes of household heads are below $30 per week and two-fifths below $20 per week, while three-fifths of all known family incomes fall below $30 per week... Some three-fifths of tenants paying less than $2.50 (rent) a week.' (18)

In general, not surprisingly, most recent local plan reports contain no information on most of these aspects.

A survey of commercial establishments may be necessary to assess the buoyancy of the area, the relationship between firms, the economic pressures on them, and their future intentions. However, once again, many important economic factors may have origins external to the area and, therefore, be difficult to ascertain. Since at least part of the success of a plan will depend upon economic realities, a good working relationship between the planning team and local firms will be essential. The kind of information needed is shown by the following quotes from the Windsor town centre plan: 'Most firms in the town have grown to their optimum size and a number are leaving the town to seek larger premises or room for expansion which is not to be found in Windsor. . . A report on shopping in Windsor carried out in 1970 by Jones, Lang & Wootton, surveyors, made particular reference to the limit to which the shopping centre could grow due to the town's restricted catchment area, the proximity to competing centres and the "old fashioned" nature of shop property in the town.' (19)

Canvassing potentially interested developers is equally important, particularly in town centre plans, and in any case where the private sector will be involved in the implementation of the plan. It is too early to assess the effects of the Community Land Act 1975, but it is likely that local authorities will henceforth control far more information at an earlier date. Planning applications, granted, pending or refused, are also a fundamental source of information of the market's intentions. Wallingford local plan is one of the few where an in-depth analysis of firms and sites has been undertaken, to assess the effects of firms on the surrounding area, the potential of vacant commercial properties, and the needs of local firms to expand. It is a good example of a combination of physical and social analysis, often lacking in other studies. (20)

The local authority's interests in the area, and that of other government agencies, has to be assessed as well. To quote the Windsor town centre plan once more: 'Recently British Rail has expressed interest in the commercial development of some of the station buildings for tourist shopping'. (21) This may have been done at the framework stage, or may have been part of the original brief; a local authority may have stated that a certain level of investment is to be directed to a local area, either by the private or the public sectors, and that a certain increase in the rate revenue is expected. It is useful to register the rateable values of the area at the moment the study starts, so as to be able to compare them with those ruling at a later date.

At the end of the analysis, factors inhibiting and contributing to change, constraints and opportunities, should have emerged. It will be possible to

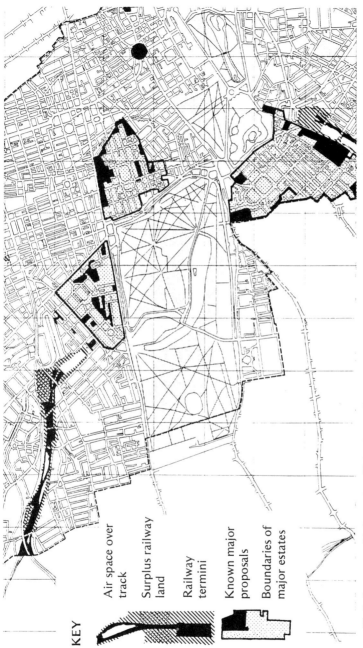

KEY

Air space over track

Surplus railway land

Railway termini

Known major proposals

Boundaries of major estates

Fig 6: Summary of Information: Major Areas of Possible Change in the City of Westminster. Source: Westminster City Council Development Plan, Report on Stage One: Problems, Issues and Priorities.

reconsider the initial appraisal of the area and to redefine the boundaries if necessary. New issues, and more important issues than those discovered initially, may have emerged, and a more precise image of the area can be established. The Manhood local plan has a heading called 'Rethinking the issues' and it is worth quoting its opening paragraph: 'On the basis of the public participation response to the form and content of the issues and the department's own consideration of the problems of the area, it was felt necessary to revise the issues. The resultant issues are worded more simply. . .' (22)

The area's problems should have been assessed in fairly certain terms and quantified whenever possible. The information should be tabulated and classified. The planning team should summarise their conclusions and make explicit what they see as the main issues in the area. A report of survey has to be produced containing these findings and including maps, tables, survey sheets, etc. This report has, by law, to be made public so that people may comment upon it and have a chance to disagree with it. It is, therefore, important that the information be presented in a manner that can be understood by the layman. Most of the quotations in this chapter come from such documents and are fairly good examples of straightforward writing.

At the beginning of this chapter, it was stated that the political and administrative structures were excluded from the overt analysis. They have to be mentioned now mainly by way of warning. Some of the information collected during the survey, or some of the results of its analysis, never get printed. It is a frequent complaint of young planners that papers they have prepared are 'doctored' by their superiors before they get to the appropriate committee or to the public. Unpleasant though this may be, it has to be accepted as a fact of political life.

## REFERENCES

1   J B McLoughlin, *Urban & regional planning: a systems approach*, Faber, 1969, p126.

2   For a wider discussion of information needs, see J B McLoughlin op cit, chapter 7, and S Chapin, *Urban land use planning*, Urbana, Illinois, 1965.

3   J Grove, 'General Improvement Areas: current practice', paper presented to Town & Country Planning Association Conference on Housing, in June 1974.

4   London Borough of Richmond upon Thames, Richmond Town Centre, Action Area Plan Report, 1976, p14, para 2.2.1.

5   East Sussex County Council and Wealden District Council, Uckfield District Plan—A Draft for Consultation, June 1976, p35, para 11.2.

6  G Burke, *Townscapes*, Penguin Books, 1976, chapter 1, p1.

7  London Borough of Richmond upon Thames, op cit, The Townscape Analysis includes maps (8 to 17.5), photographs and written text (para 22) and is a major part of the report (pp14-41).

8  S Pembroke, An Indpendent Synopsis—Summary of Objections made at the Local Public Inquiry on the Covent Garden CDA, July 6-Sept 16 1971, p27 quoting first the Chief Planner and then an objector.

9  J N Jackson, *Surveys for town and country planning*, London, 1962. J B McLoughlin, op cit.

10  T L C Duncan, *Measuring housing quality*, University of Birmingham, Centre for Urban and Regional Studies, Occasional Paper no 20, 1971.

11  East Sussex C C and Wealden D C, op cit para 10.16, p29.

12  City of Coventry, Eagle Street Action Area Plan, Written Statement, April 1975, para 2.09, p3.

13  London Borough of Richmond upon Thames, op cit, para 2.4.2, p48.

14  H Gans, *People and plans*, Basic Books, New York, 1968.

15  City of Coventry, op cit, Appendix to Statement on Publicity and Public Participation, June 1975.  Appendix D, Exhibition Panels—Social Survey.

16  K Lynch, *The image of the city*, MIT Press, 1960.  P R Gould and R R White, *Mental maps*, Penguin Books, 1971.  B Goodey, *Perception of the environment: an introduction to the literature*, University of Birmingham, Centre for Urban and Regional Studies, 1971.

17  City of Coventry, op cit, para 2.16 p5.

18  City of Coventry, op cit, Appendix B, Social Survey, abridged results, para 2.2.

19  Berkshire County Council and the Royal Borough of Windsor and Maidenhead, Windsor Town Centre Draft Plan, part 6.4.1, p23 and para 8.2.1, p35.  These comments have not been reprinted in the final version of the District Plan.

20  South Oxfordshire District Council, District Plan for Wallingford, Draft Local Plan, Jan 1976, paras 4.3 to 4.5.5, pp31-36 and section 6, pp51-61.

21  Berkshire C C and the Royal Borough of Windsor and Maidenhead, op cit, para 6.7.5, p26.

22  Chichester District Council, Manhood Local Plan, Feb 1976, Interim Report of Survey, part 1, para 2.1, p6.

Chapter 4

# PUBLIC PARTICIPATION, GOALS AND OBJECTIVES

In this chapter, various stages of public participation, the specification of goals and the formulation of objectives will be treated as separate items. In the real world of day-to-day planning, it is unlikely that they will be so clearly separated. In particular, the public participation process should be seen as a continuous one, and only for analytical purposes will it be presented here as having separate steps.

### Participation or consultation?
Public participation is a subject that has been talked about and discussed *ad nauseam* in the last ten years. Reactions to the practice of it have changed from resistance by local authority officers and welcome from action groups, to almost the exact reverse: today, local authorities in general have adopted and accept some form of public participation, even though not always wholeheartedly, while action groups often dismiss it as a waste of time. All the pros and cons of public participation cannot be discussed here, but some important points have to be outlined before considering the local planning implications.

To start with, it must be recognised that nothing, or practically nothing, that has been done in Britain represents real participation—which means sharing: 'We understand participation to be the act of sharing in the formulation of policies and proposals'. (1)

If we take S Arnstein's *Ladder of citizen participation*, which found twelve participatory steps from 'manipulation' through 'consultation' and 'placation' to 'citizen control', it will be seen that the top levels of the ladder have never been reached. (2) Public meetings, exhibitions, leafleting, house-to-house interviews, are all public participation exercises; but they do not add up to sharing in the decision-making process. There may be good reasons for this—some commentators blame the planners and some the public. It may be that total participation is an unattainable goal; that nobody really wants it; or indeed, that it would be harmful. It seems, though, that part of the present frustration and resentment stems from the use of the terminology: everyone talks about participation but nobody practises it. 'Consultation' or 'public discussion' would, therefore, describe more accurately what is being done.

At an East of England RTPI Branch meeting on Local Plans and the Public, it was interesting to listen to a GLC officer equating public relations to public participation: 'The planned effort to establish and improve the degree of mutual understanding between an organisation or any individual and any groups of persons or organisation with the primary object of assisting that organisation or individual to deserve, acquire and maintain the good reputation.' (3) No comment is needed!

At the same meeting, P Stringer, from the University of Sheffield, listed the three main objectives of public participation as being:

Dispersal of information;

Collection of information;

Enhancement of citizenship;

and pointed out that different techniques should be applied to achieve each of them. (4) Whilst this list does not include the top echelons of Arnstein's ladder, it is realistic and gives an honest description of what participation is in this country.

A different and rather cynical point of view was expressed by Alan Howard of the Ramblers Association in *The planner* of September 1976: 'Instead of arguing endlessly about participation, it would be better if all concerned recognised the futility of it and agreed to go back to its well-tried, time-honoured predecessor—confrontation.' (5)

These comments do not negate the possibility that public participation could exist, but they show that it demands a commitment which the elected representatives (who, after all, have been elected to represent and not to relinquish their collectively delegated powers), their officers (who are paid to give advice based on expertise and have to show they know better) and the public at large (which votes reluctantly and has better things to do anyway) are unwilling to make at this time.

Colin Fudge, of the School of Advanced Urban Studies in Bristol, has suggested on the basis of a slightly modified version of the three main objectives quoted above that to achieve interaction with the public, planners have to get through the other stages of dispersal and collection of information, and he illustrated this as a 'Public participation' box (see figure 7). He sees the achievement of the interaction as an educational process, which will obviously not be immediate. In the meantime, he classifies the public into: major elite; minor elite; general public as a mass.

At the moment, planners address themselves mainly to the first two groups. (6) Members of the general public who try to participate, usually develop into a minor élite, an example is that of the squatters whose activities, most of the time, result in confrontation, but occasionally achieve a certain degree of real participation.

Fig 7: Colin Fudge's 'Public participation maze'.

53

## Initial stages of public participation

The 1971 Town & Country Planning Act requires a local planning authority proposing to prepare a local plan to ensure that:

'a) adequate publicity is given in their area to any relevant matter arising out of a survey of the area carried out by them under section 6 of this Act and to matters proposed to be included in the plan;

b) that persons who may be expected to desire an opportunity of making representations to the authority with respect to those matters are made aware that they are entitled to an opportunity of doing so; and

c) that such persons are given an adequate opportunity of making such representations; and the authority shall consider any representations made to them within the prescribed period.' (7)

It is, however, in the interest of the authorities and the public to start the process as soon as the decision has been taken to produce a local plan for an area; this intention should be made public and those who have an interest in the area should be asked to voice their demands for the area. The boundaries of the area may not have been finally determined and, therefore, people from a wider area than that which the final local plan will cover, may have to be involved.

Several methods can be used to approach this stage: referring back again to the three objectives outlined by P Stringer, the techniques related to each of them are as follows:
Dispersal of information: mass media, leaflets, exhibitions, public meetings.
Collection of information: surveys, study groups, forms, consultative groups.
Enhancement of citizenship: political structure, forums, co-option on committees. (8)

Each of the systems adopted has its advantages and drawbacks. With regard to public meetings, for example, it may be difficult at this stage to get a response from the public, since there is very little they can yet react to. An area of North Islington had been chosen by the council for an experimental housing action area, before the publication of the Act on the subject. The area has already been surveyed by an action group sponsored by Shelter, and the residents, supposedly, had expressed considerable concern about the local conditions. About 800 letters were distributed personally by the planning team through every door in the area, inviting people to a meeting in the local school to discuss the future of the area; but careful to avoid giving the impression that any proposal existed. Only fifty people turned up, and this figure included outsiders, students and social workers who had been attracted to the meeting by the publicity the scheme was having! Had the letter been worded in a more provocative way, implying some threat to homes, more people would probably have turned up, even though they would have accused the council of taking decisions behind their backs.

With regard to exhibitions combined with forms to be filled in, the response can be mixed. If the exhibition is slick, people may complain
54

**Tower Hamlets Planner**

TOWER HAMLETS COUNCIL PLANNING BULLETIN

Council asks residents—

"Tell us what you want to see in your area"

# PLANNING THE FUTURE CUBITT TOWN

Tower Hamlets Council has prepared outline proposals for the Cubitt Town

Mudchute: Today the children play, tomorrow ...

**Committee to loo[k] Docklands as who[le]**

ঈগল স্ট্রীট অ্যাকশন এরিয়ার খবর

# EAGLE STREET ACTION AREA NEWS

NEWSLETTER No. 1

WHERE IS EAGLE STREET ACTION AREA?

WHAT IS AN ACTION AREA?

WHY HAVE AN ACTION AREA?

WHY HAVE THIS NEWSLETTER?

HOW CAN RESIDENTS BECOME INVOLVED?

**WHAT DO YOU THINK?**

Fig. 8: Examples of public participation leaflets.

55

that the council's mind has been made up beforehand and that their own comments are irrelevant. If it is sketchy and simply asks people what they would like, people's reaction may be 'Why ask us? You are the professionals, you should know!' The location of an exhibition is fundamental to its success: people will not make a special effort to go to it; they have to find it on their way whilst undertaking some other usual activity such as shopping.

Some of the problems associated with social surveys have already been mentioned. The way and circumstances in which questions are put to the public, and the way people react to certain questions, can influence the answers: the same person may answer differently at a public meeting, where she knows she has an audience, from the way she answers a written questionnaire or an interviewer at her doorstep. In all cases, the interpretation of the answers will not be easy; and it is important to listen to all types of requests from the people, not only those related to town-planning directly. For the members of the public, the local authority is a unity and not a series of separate departments; comments or complaints are made to the council in general. The report on a GIA in Cambridge, for instance, states: 'Curiously enough, the main issues that originally came up did not necessarily need great improvement area action. They were repair of streets and footpaths; getting on with the promised housing on a ten year old cleared site; and doing something about the derelict houses nearly all owned by the council. . . Anyone wanting a gold medal for "improving" an area should keep clear of this degree of participation.' (9)

In this particular case, a local committee of representatives was formed with sixteen members, each of them representing a group of about fifteen houses. It met together with the ward councillors in someone's living room. Members of the planning team were also present. The report indicates that, not only has this exercise been successful in terms of the relationship between planners and those planned for, but that it has even saved money for the council in terms of staff time and capital costs. This method and the area-based office are increasingly favoured by local authorities. In the case of local forums, it is important to inform all other interested parties of what is going on at its meetings: otherwise they will feel left out. This is probably one of the failures of the Covent Garden Forum, a group representing all the interests in the area and meeting with officers and councillors to discuss the future of the Covent Garden area. Because of the lack of feedback to the area, residents have completely lost faith in the forum and tend to consider it as remote and autocratic as the GLC. (10)

One problem in any public participation exercise, which is often used to condemn all such exercises, occurs particularly at the early stages: how can we ensure that whatever response is received is representative of the area as a whole? It can be argued that this is impossible to achieve

56

or that it does not matter anyway. In areas with a variety of activities and land-uses, this problem is indeed very difficult to resolve. The case of Covent Garden offers once again a good example: the area includes residents of long standing and newcomers, traditional businesses and new traders, theatres, artisans, light industry, etc. The local action group, the Covent Garden Community Association, which successfully fought the original plan proposed by the GLC, is intended to represent all the various interest groups. Although these were united in the initial fight, divisions started as soon as alternative proposals had to be put forward, and sub-groups attacked one another as being non-representative. (11) Later, the forum was elected, also to represent all interests. Then, after a year of collaboration, the CGCA barred its officers from sitting on the forum. Furthermore, in view of the role and location of Covent Garden, it could be argued that all Londoners should be consulted about its future.

Planners will have to do their best to identify representative groups and involve them from the outset, but if people do not react against a particular group, it can reasonably be assumed that they consider it as representative.

### Initial definition of goals

At a very early stage in the process, before any systematic analysis of the area has been undertaken, broad goals have to be defined, which will give a 'raison d'être' for the plan.

If the corresponding structure plan has been completed, goals for the local area may have been specified; alternatively, regional or county policies may exist which, at least implicitly, set out goals for the local area. The people in charge of the plan preparation, ie the planner in the wider sense of the word (which includes politicians and professionals other than town-planners), will have at least an impressionistic view of the area and will have drawn some conclusions about what the more obvious problems are. If the process of public participation has started, certain demands or complaints will have already been voiced.

The level of abstraction or detail of these initial goals is difficult to decide. Although they may be non-operational, these goals must summarise what the plan sets out to achieve—as understood at this time. Statements such as: 'to make the area a better place in which to live and work' might have some value in a political campaign, but are of no use in planning terms. Practically any policy action would achieve these vague aims and they, therefore, could not be used to test the comparative value of different proposals. On the other hand, if they are too precise, they may be the wrong ones; they may orientate the plan in the wrong direction; and they may be criticised for pre-empting conclusions. A delicate balance has, therefore, to be achieved of goals that are general enough, yet include some amount of intention of policy in them. It is also important that these goals be made explicit and publicised, so that they can be discussed at a very early stage and amended if necessary.

The following are two examples of goals set for the original plan for Covent Garden, as early as 1966:

'a) The incorporation of a complex of uses to create a vigorous and interesting environment by day and by night both as a place to live and as a centre for entertainment and cultural activities.' (12) Although this may be seen as a commendable goal, it can mean all things to all people. If the area had been left exactly as it was, it would have responded to the goal; if it has been razed to the ground and rebuilt, it could also have fulfilled the goal. Furthermore, the quoted goal uses the word 'incorporate', which seems to ignore the fact that those uses listed already existed within the area. It could be argued that since a further goal expressed the intention to retain the character of the area, the possibility of razing the area to the ground had been dismissed. However, the plan's proposals took precisely that kind of alternative!

'b) A substantial increase in residential accommodation.' (13) This is possibly a goal that nobody would argue against. However, what does 'substantial' mean? Since it is not qualified, can it be assumed that any kind of residential accommodation would be equally desirable? It can be argued that as long as the principle is accepted, this is all that is needed at this stage, leaving the details to be worked out later; or that this is all that should concern the planners. But it may also be that the qualifications of the goal are of fundamental and significant importance; and that, therefore, the goal may be acceptable only if these further details are known. For example, the above goal could have been qualified by saying: 'An increase in residential accommodation related to low income groups needing accommodation in the area, and to the opportunities offered by the available supporting services.' This would still allow for details to be worked out at a later stage, but it would give firmer terms of reference.

### Formulation of objectives and further stages of public participation

As stated earlier, once the relevant information about the area has been collected and the local situation has been analysed, a report of survey with the planners conclusions has to be made public. To be useful, it should contain a description of the area's problems and opportunities, whenever possible in quantified terms. This report is then to be tested through a second exercise in public participation—in other words, the people involved should be asked whether they agree with the report's conclusions. If the public has been continuously involved during the survey stages, there should be no surprises; but there may be various interest groups which view the area's situation differently from the authority. The common reaction to the environmental health inspector condemning a

58

house as unfit is a classic one that exemplifies the different attitudes taken by planners and the public; and it is one that is repeatedly heard at public meetings:

'I have kept my house in good order, it is well decorated and we have lived in it very happily for all these years. How can you say it is unfit?'

Just as the problems should be expressed in quantified form, the original goals should now be turned into specific operational objectives of the kind:

'To provide domestic facilities in a self-contained unit to every household in the area.'

'To have a public transport stop at no more than two minutes walk from each dwelling.'

'To avoid the intrusion of through traffic into the area.'

Unfortunately, published plans remain vague, possibly to avoid commitments. Compare the second objective above to the following one from the Richmond town centre plan: 'To provide a high degree of accessibility for public transport and the servicing of premises.'

How high is high? Similarly, in the next example from the same plan, how can the authority know when the objective has been achieved? 'To improve and increase the housing available and to favour in particular those changes and improvements which will benefit the existing population.'

On the other hand, objectives should not be confused with policies or proposals. The basic difference is that in general, there are several policies that could fulfil one objective. The following, also from the Richmond plan gives no possibility of alternatives and cannot really be accepted as an objective: 'To provide a site for a cultural centre.' (14) It is a statement of policy satisfying an objective of the kind: 'to ensure that cultural activities can be developed in an adequate form'.

Not all problems and objectives can be quantified, and not all are simple and easy to interpret. In particular, those concerned with the aesthetic or sensorial quality of the environment are basically subjective and might be interpreted in different forms:

'To achieve high standards of environmental design.'

'To maintain and enhance areas of townscape which give distinctive local character.'

The kind of objectives illustrated by these two examples appear in many local plans; and although they are very general, it is difficult to see how they could be made more precise. Techniques have been developed to try to convert these into measurable objectives, and some progress has been achieved in relation to noise and air pollution, but not much in aesthetic issues.

The public debate on the report of survey and the formulation of objectives should go hand in hand; ideally, the planners and their client should have worked together throughout, to evolve a list of objectives derived from the problems considered. In practice, the process is not always smooth, and consensus will only exceptionally have been achieved. After the failure of their first plan, the GLC team for Covent Garden started an exercise of this kind. Papers on various issues affecting the area were distributed to interested parties; a summary of conclusions and a questionnaire were attached, and people were asked to complete and return the latter. The answers would then allow the team to deduce operational objectives. The following are examples of questions in one of the papers, *Living in Covent Garden*:

'It is said that there are not enough shops for the present population, which shops do you miss?'

'Should the number and choice of shops be increased in the future?' (15)

Unfortunately, some of the questions were worded in such a manner that they were almost impossible for a layman to answer—the examples above were followed by the question: 'How can this be done?'

It is almost certain that conflicting objectives will emerge. Not only will different groups have differing objectives, but also within one group various objectives may be incompatible with each other. The following statement in the Wallingford district plan, following a public meeting, is surprising and disappointing: 'It was particularly useful because there seemed to be a firm consensus on the major issues and statements made at the end of the meeting provided the Working Party with clear guidelines within which to work.' (16)

What profile of the public is being consulted will certainly influence the answers and therefore the degree of consensus or conflict. Chichester District Council undertook a fairly extensive public participation exercise for their Manhood plan—public meetings, exhibitions, questionnaires, a community forum; all of these involved local residents and, not surprisingly, some of the resulting objectives were:

Agricultural land should be sacrosant.

Local needs should always come before those of tourists. (17)

The chances are that if they had also consulted visitors or potential visitors to the area, or people looking for houses to retire to on the coast, the answers would have been different. Furthermore, at this stage, conflicts between the goals set at strategic level and those emerging at local level, will become obvious.

Two questions are important in relation to these potential conflicts: the first, a technical one—how to discover or predict the conflicts—is fairly easy. The other, how to solve the conflicts, is not only much more complicated but is basically political, and cannot be given a clear answer here. Planners can only expose the conflicts and show how the various objectives reflect the interests of various groups. To test the compatibility

60

of various objectives, the goals compatibility matrix can be used, which will also allow the objectives to be put in some order of priorities. Another kind of matrix (Table 3) can be used to compare and discover conflicts and compatibilities between objectives of various groups.

| Group eg | GR 1 Central government | GR 2 Local authority | GR 3 Residents area A | GR 4 Residents area B | GR n |
|---|---|---|---|---|---|
| Subject/ system | | | | | |
| Housing | Objective 1.1 | Obj 2.1 | Obj 3.1 | Obj 4.1 | Obj n.1 |
| | Obj 1.2 | Obj 2.2 | Obj 3.2 | Obj 4.2 | Obj n.2 |
| | Obj 1.3 | | | | |
| Shopping | Obj 1.4 | | | | |
| Transport | Obj 1.5 | | etc | | |
| Environment | Obj 1.6 | | | | |
| etc | Obj 1.n | | | | |

Table 3: Group objectives compatibility matrix

A well known example of conflicts between objectives at strategic level and those of local areas is that of the London Motorway box. In the mid-sixties the principle of the need for a major ring road network was generally accepted, for transportation reasons, at strategic level. When considered at local level, it appeared to be totally incompatible with housing, environmental and other objectives, and ran into so much local opposition that its validity at strategic level had to be reconsidered and the scheme was finally abandoned. A similar case was that of London's projected third airport. (18)

Potential clashes between local and super-local objectives will arise fairly often, and have to be solved at the political level. They can, however, be a source of disatisfaction and disaffection, since it is difficult to explain to members of the public that, though they were asked to participate in the planning process, there are some issues which have been pre-empted by higher level decisions. More subtle conflicts than those previously quoted (and, therefore, more difficult to resolve) may also appear. It is to be noted that the local planning reports which we have considered, only very rarely describe the conflicts that have arisen. The situation is particularly delicate when local plans are being prepared in parallel with the structure plan; but it also has the advantage that both levels have still a certain degree of flexibility, and can influence one another, before positions have been taken. The work in South Hampshire, both at county and district levels, should be examined for a good indication of possible approaches to this situation. (19)

In general terms, the only way that the various conflicts might be solved will be through exposing them and opening them for public debate. No absolute consensus is ever likely to be reached, but at least differences will be aired and some form of compromise may be achieved. Then possibly, at the end of this stage, the planning team will have a set of clear objectives for the area, in some order of priority, or with certain weightings.

### Evaluation and later stages of public participation

After the planning team has prepared alternative proposals for the area, these have to be compared and evaluated in relation to the agreed objectives. Various techniques exist for this and are mentioned in the next chapter.

The various alternatives, and the results of the technical evaluation, should be made public and opened to comment and discussion. A much wider response should be achieved at this stage, since people's lives can now be seen to be directly affected by the proposals. The same problems mentioned before—of how representative is the response, of finding the right way to get to the public, and of involving as many people as possible—continue to exist.

The main problem will be how to communicate the proposals in a comprehensible and interesting way: the public's attention has to be attracted, they have to understand the proposals and their relevance. If the proposals are presented in jargon and deal with abstract concepts rather than day-to-day realities, they will only alienate the public. The plan has to speak to the people about their local area and their own lives, regardless of whether or not this falls neatly within the town and country planning legislation and the planners technical language. However, potted versions of the technical report, specially prepared for public consumption, can often be misleading because of what is omitted. Proposals should be as concrete as possible, even when presented as alternatives to be decided upon.

People should be made aware that in choosing, they are trading one thing for another. For instance, within a specific economic and financial context, two alternative proposals relating to the residential environment may include: one, the maintenance of low housing density; the other, the introduction of a public transport system. It may not be ovbious to the layman that these two policies are incompatible, and this should be made clear if it has not already been done at the stage of formulating objectives. The local authority is entitled to indicate which is its

Fig. 9: Public Participation literature: presenting choices to the public.

preferred strategy, but the information should be presented in an unbiased form. The public has to be reassured that the local authority has not taken the decision beforehand, and that their comments will be taken into account. Following the public consultation in Eagle Street mentioned above, the local residents' association submitted their own housing proposals and, 'after careful study of the residents' plan, the council considered that a number of the proposals contained therein offered both practicable and possible solutions to problems in the area. Where it was felt that these proposals were consistent with local needs and city-wide needs in some cases, they have been incorporated in the final plan for the area'. (20) Note the mention of 'city-wide' needs as a source of possible conflict.

Various methods have been tried to bring alternatives and evaluations to the public, none too successfully. It can, however, be hoped that if people have been involved with the plan right from the beginning, their awareness and interest should be greater than it has been in the past, and they should have achieved a good level of communication with the planners. The argument that public participation takes time and complicates the life of the planners, should not be an excuse for not trying.

### Final stage of participation: the public inquiry

Once the local plan has been completed, and assuming the corresponding structure plan has been approved, the document is to be put on deposit for inspection by the public and time allowed for objections to be made to it. A copy of it is sent to the Secretary of State, together with a statement explaining what the local authority has done in relation to public participation and what notice it has taken of people's comments. If the Secretary of State is not satisfied that the local authority has complied with the legislation, he can stop the procedures at this point and direct the authority to comply with it. Otherwise, the objections to the local plan are to be considered at a 'local public inquiry'. There is a minimum period of six weeks after submission of the plan for members of the public to lodge objections. Another six weeks must be allowed between the notice of the inquiry and the inquiry itself; this period can be used for discussions between the authority and the objectors, which often solve a number of difficulties.

As opposed to the public inquiries held for the previous development plans, or the examination in public for a structure plan, this one is not controlled by the Secretary of State. It will be chaired by an independent inspector from the DOE, but his report is sent to the local authority. Up to now, only a few such public inquiries have taken place—that into the Eagle Street plan in Coventry was the first one. The rules for the procedures were published in late 1977 *Local plans, public local inquiries: a guide to procedure*. It is intended to be relaxed and fairly informal and, maybe for that reason, this first inquiry was held in a bingo hall. At the end of the inquiry, the inspector reports to the local authority, which may have to modify the plan as a result. The cost of the inquiry is borne by the local authority.

Even after an optimum process of participation, it is unlikely that no objections will be forthcoming: in the case of Eagle Street, 347 objections were received in spite of the efforts by the council to involve the public throughout. However, if the communications between planners and those planned for worked properly, the objections at this stage may relate to interests damaged by the proposals and not to matters of principle. In the case of the recent Covent Garden plan, most of the objections had been aired before the inquiry—this was very well organised and only dealt with matters of detail.

The authority does not have to justify the plan, since it is conducting the inquiry to scrutinise the objections:

'The object of the inquiry is to examine the objections to the proposals in a way that allows the planning authority to reach conclusions about them.'

'The inspector's objectives are to find out and record the relevant facts; to report to the planning authority on the objections as presented to him; to set out his views on the merits of the objections; and to make recommendations about modifications to the plan.' (21)

After consideration of the inspector's report, and if the plan conforms with the structure plan, it can be adopted by the local authority. The Secretary of State has reserved powers to approve the plans or to make directions, but these should be used only in exceptional cases. (22)

Ideally, neither the planning process nor the participation by the public will end here. Throughout implementation of the proposals, there should still be public involvement, even though it is not required by law. This will be discussed in a later chapter.

## REFERENCES

1  Department of the Environment, *People and planning—report of the Committee on Public Participation in Planning*, HMSO, London, 1969. Introduction, para 5a, p1.

2  S R Arnstein, 'A ladder of citizen participation,' in the *Journal of the American Institute of Planners*, 35, July 1969, pp216-224.

3  East of England Branch of the Royal Town Planning Institute. Meeting on Local Plans and Public, Nov 21, 1975; Geoff Lewis, Information Officer of the Greater London Council.

4  See P Stringer and G Plumridge, 'Linked Research Project into Public Participation in Structure Planning'. Interim Research Paper No 1, 1974, Publicity and Communication Media in Structure Planning.

5  A Howard, 'The great participation fallacy', in *The planner*, vol 62, no 6, p164, Sept 1976.

6  C Fudge, lecturer at the School for Advanced Urban Studies, University of Bristol, Course on Local Plans, April 1978.

7  Town & Country Planning Act 1971, c78, S12(1).  See also Town & Country Planning (Structure and Local Plans) Regulations 1974; Town & Country Planning (Local Plans for Greater London) Regulations 1974 and DOE Circular 55/77, paras 3.42–3.49.

8  P Stringer and G Plumridge, op cit. There are at present fourteen Interim Research Papers published as part of the research project.

9  R Darlington, *Public participation in practice: experience in a general improvement area in the back streets of Cambridge*, Cambridge City Council, 1975, pp2 and 3.

10  The Covent Garden Forum first elected in June 1974 by residents, workers, students from locally based colleges, and owners of business or property in the area, has thirty members representing the various interests in the area.  It meets every three weeks and is now elected every two years.  See the Greater London Council (Covent Garden) GLC Action Area Plan, 1978, p12.

11  The vice-chairman of the Covent Garden Community Association said in November 1976: 'I also believe, that the CGCA should play its role in *opposing* the Forum as it is presently set up . . . the Forum cannot operate as a successful representative of Covent Garden'.

12  Consortium of Greater London Council, Westminster City Council and London Borough of Camden, Covent Garden's Moving, Covent Garden Area Draft Plan, 1968.  Brief, para 9, p10.

13  As above.

14  London Borough of Richmond upon Thames, Richmond Town Centre, Action Area Plan Report, 1976.  The three quotes are from chapter 3, Aims and Objectives, p54, no 9, 19 and 11.

15  Covent Garden Development Team, Covent Garden Local Plan, Report of Survey, Discussion Paper No 2, Living in Covent Garden, June 1974.  The questionnaires were given separately, but together with the discussion papers.

16  South Oxfordshire District Council, District Plan for Wallingford, Draft Local Plan, Jan 1976, para 1.6, p8.

17  Chichester District Council, Manhood Local Plan, First Report on Public Participation, December 1975, para 4.1, p6 and para 8.1, p12.

18  See for instance: D A Hart, *Strategic planning in London, the rise and fall of the primary road network*, Pergamon Press, Oxford, 1976; and 'Transport strategy in London', presented as evidence by LATA at

the Public Inquiry into the GLDP, Jan 1971. And also, O Cook, *The Stansted affair*, Pan Books, 1967.

19  R Brown, 'Linking local planning with structure planning', *The planner*, vol 60, no 1, Jan 1974, p505.

20  City of Coventry, Eagle Street Action Area Plan, Written Statement, April 1975, p9, para 4.01.

21  Local Plans: Public Local Inquiries, A Guide to Procedure, DOE, 1977, para 3.26, p20, and para 3.29, p21.

22  The longest public inquiry into a local planning has been that for the Fareham Western Wards Action Area: eleven weeks and 218 modifications to the original plan.

Chapter 5

# PLAN GENERATION IN LOCAL PLANNING

The local area has now, in our cycle of progress, been thoroughly analysed,
a large amount of information about it has been collected and digested,
a number of objectives has been agreed. A 'plan' should now be produced,
reflecting the results of the previous stages.

A wide gap exists at this point between the research parts of the process
and the design phase—if the word 'design' can be used in the widest sense
to include the conceptual process that takes place. There exist similarities here with what architects have to do between getting their client's
brief and making a survey of the site on the one hand, and their design
of the required building on the other. It would be pleasant to believe that
if all the information and the objectives were fed into a computer, a plan
would emerge at the other end. (1) Unfortunately, the reality is never
so simple.

## Alternative strategies

It would be pointless to have gone through the previous phases of the
process if the final product did not reflect these. The planner should,
therefore, start by considering each of the objectives the plan has to satisfy
and the related information.

With the opportunities and constraints as known quantities, it is likely
that each objective could be satisfied by a variety of policy solutions;
ideally, as many of these as possible should be put forward. It has been
argued that it is pointless to work out alternatives which are unrealistic,
but at this stage what is realistic or not may not be known: what appears
to be unlikely of implementation today, may become feasible tomorrow.
In any case, the planner's experience should be sufficient to filter alternatives which are totally absurd; the more imaginative the proposals at
this stage, the more likely that a satisfactory answer will be found.
Additionally, solutions to one set of problems can often be found almost
by accident in a different field to the one originally considered.

At this stage, not all alternatives will relate to land-use planning.
Indeed, there is no reason why they should, since not all the problems
identified, nor all the objectives, will have been physical ones. Action on
those proposals may be the concern of departments other than the planning

**Barnsley Town Centre Action Area Plan**

## PROPOSALS MAP 1B
## LAND USE POLICIES

Boundary of action area

**Predominant Use Areas**

- [1] Huddersfield Road / Victoria Road office area (B8-10)
- [2] Central office area (B11)
- [3] Central shopping area (S11-13)
- [4] South Western industrial area (IN6-7)
- [5] Eastern industrial area (IN6-7)
- [6] Northern housing area (H6-7)
- [7] Joseph Street housing area (H8)

▼▼▼▼ Shopping frontages (S10)

**Mixed Use Areas**

- [8] Blucher Street / Castlereagh Street area (M1-4)
- [9] York Street / George Street area (M5-7)
- [10] Doncaster Road fringe area (M8-11)
- [11] Churchfields / Church Street area (M12-13)
- [12] Town End (M14)
- [13] Harborough Hill (M15)
- [14] Passenger transport interchange (M16)

Proposal T32 also relates to the central shopping area

Scale 1:5000

Fig 10: A proposals map showing land-use policies on various sites: Barnsley Town Centre Draft Action Area Plan.
Source: Barnsley Metropolitan District Council.

department; and this is where the importance of the corporate approach to local planning is put in evidence, and where multi-departmental teams have a fundamental role to play. In a note on the role of local plans, the DOE has stated: 'Local plans are land-use plans. They cannot be used to implement non-land-use aspects of social policies although they will form the statutory land-use element of district corporate plans.' (2)

This very narrow-minded approach can only be explained by the power of bureaucracy and its resulting compartmentalisation. Not surprisingly, R Hambleton, in an article in *The planner* of September 1976, stated: 'Many of the most promising experiments in area-based policy-making and management seem to be happening despite local planning and not because of it.' (3)

The success of a local plan does not stem from the creation of a beautiful document which lays down land-uses and development policies. It must relate directly to the problems of the area considered, going, if necessary, beyond the strict definitions of the Town & Country Planning Acts and responding to identified client groups. If the DOE insists on having exclusively land-use local plans, local authorities would be well advised to produce other comprehensive plans from which they would extract the land-use aspects for submission to the Ministry. This is, in fact, what the DOE seems to have suggested in their more recent Note 1/78, which states on the one hand: 'A designated planning authority pursuing a comprehensive policy approach to the problems of an area may wish to combine this approach with preparation of a local plan.' And on the other hand: 'Any related but non-planning activities should be referred to in the reasoned justification where necessary, but must not be distinguished as proposals nor shown on the proposals map.' (4)

If the planning team has been involved with the people in the area throughout the process, and if it includes people from all the local authority's service departments, there should be no difficulty at this stage; policies proposed would automatically relate to physical aspects as well as social, economic and managerial factors. The following example illustrates the wide range of alternatives that can be suggested to solve the relatively simple problems of an area of poor housing. An area in North Islington had the following problems: poor housing conditions (both in structure and lack of facilities), multi-occupation and overcrowding, combined with under-occupation; low incomes and lack of public open space. The main physical opportunity was provided by two neighbouring sites which were owned by statutory undertakers who would dispose of them in the near future. The agreed objectives were:

To provide each household with a self-contained dwelling with all facilities;

To avoid displacing people from the area if they wished to remain;

To minimise any increase in rents;

70

To improve the environment and provide some local open space.
Possible solutions to the area's problems could be:
Redevelopment of the whole area by the council;
Redevelopment of the worst housing by the council;
A rolling programme of redevelopment by the council;
Compulsory purchase and improvement of all properties by the council;
Compulsory purchase and improvement by the council of those ten-anted properties in bad condition and/or badly managed;
Declaring the area a GIA (this was in pre-housing Action Area days);
Building on the available sites and rehousing tenants from the worst conditions;
Acquiring and improving those properties that came on the market;
Serving improvement notices;
Using the available sites to provide public open space, etc.

The list is certainly not comprehensive, and it includes only fairly traditional alternatives that fall within the town-planning, housing, or public health legislation. However, it shows the importance of collaboration between various departments and the sharing of knowledge about what is feasible. In the above proposals, the departments and committees dealing with planning, housing, health, recreation and architecture were involved. According to DOE's instructions, local plans would only include town-planning policies, and refer to the others, which can only lead to confusion.

On the other hand, though it is important to consider possible alternatives, it is not necessary to 'invent' them when they do not really exist. To satisfy statutory requirements and professional fashion, some planning departments have included a series of proposals which are feasible, and then made up variations which are known to be impractical, only to be able to abandon the latter at a subsequent stage.

There must be a careful analysis of the alternatives to assess their compatibility, feasibility and degree of comprehensiveness. Some will be found to be impractical; some will be incompatible with each other, and others will solve more than one problem or fulfil more than one objective. Alternatives which are isolated (ie, do not relate to more than one topic) and which are not very different from the objectives, should be avoided. Too often, plans show a series of alternatives based on topics, yet further on the proposals for specific areas are not seen in terms of alternatives at all. The team will, therefore, have to consider alternatives in more than one dimension—on a topic basis and on an area basis.

The Manhood plan is a welcome example: 'So far this report has examined planning policies on a topic by topic basis. While this approach is a convenient means of analysis, it is somewhat artificial in that the various policies do not exist or work independently. It is equally important to know how the various policies work together to influence the development of an area.' (5)

71

In this plan, each issue is first considered in general, and the feasibility and desirability of each proposal is then analysed in relation to specific sub-areas. To return to the previous example of North Islington, the alternatives cannot be limited to redevelopment-versus-rehabilitation and then sites designated for one or the other; each site has to be considered in relation to others and within itself, and a comparison between various actions and land-uses discussed. Techniques for this part of the process have been applied mainly at the strategic level: see for instance Friend and Jessop's *Local government and strategic choice*, or the Nottingham-Derbyshire sub-regional study. (6) The plan for the Manhood is exceptional in having tried to apply the techniques to a district plan. Another, more recent document, the Barnsley town centre draft Action Area plan, follows a similar method; it puts forward a number of proposals by topic and then discusses their application to specific sites in a detailed way: 'Proposals which apply to specific parts of the town centre are included under the appropriate topic where the predominant use of the specific area is the same as the topic. The last section of proposals includes proposals applied to specific areas where no one use predominates. Each proposal is cross-referenced to the main points in the reasoned justification relating to the proposal.' (7) Additionally a series of maps illustrate these proposals.

### Choice of the 'best alternative'
The analysis of alternatives should generally produce a limited number of valid alternative solutions, combined in packages and relating to, if not always fulfilling, the various objectives. These should now be put in front of the public and be open to debate. The previous chapter discussed public participation in the process, and from this and from a further analysis of the alternatives, a final choice of solutions should be arrived at. This may be one of the proposed packages of alternatives, in its original form or modified, a combination of two or more alternatives, or with the inclusion of new proposals. A solution that takes into account the objectives of the various groups involved should then be chosen. It is more than likely that it will not satisfy everybody equally; but it is to be hoped that it will not be one that does not satisfy anyone, as is sometimes the case with compromises.

The planning team can now develop this chosen alternative into a draft plan which will include all kinds of policies, whether physical, socio-economic or managerial, even though the purely town-planning part of it will relate mainly to detailed land-uses, criteria for development control and, in some cases, for design control, traffic and transport policies, programming of public investment and development, and the related phasing of private development. The Town & Country Planning Regulations 1974 list the subject matters that might be included: population
72

and employment, housing, industry and commerce, etc; that is to say, the standard topics included in any comprehensive planning document. (8) As already mentioned, to be of interest to the people concerned, the chosen alternative must be seen to relate to the problems and objectives perceived by the community, and, therefore, should include a package of proposals that go beyond this straitjacket of the traditional land-use divisions.

Taking this last point to its extreme, T MacMurray suggested that having identified problems from the perspective of client groups, the planner 'will tend to develop packages of policies and programmes for each group. The "core" of each package will be policies and plans for physical change, complemented by a series of back-up social and financial services, as necessary.' (9) But the difficulties in administering such schemes for client groups would be numerous, and the fragmentation that would result could be destructive. It should be possible to integrate within one plan policies which affect various interest groups, deal with more than purely physical issues and involve all the relevant local authority's departments.

It is axiomatic that the several practicable alternatives will have been costed and appraised in financial terms; the resources available and the costs have to be matched and the prospective contributions of the public and private sectors made as explicit as possible at the evaluation stage. It should be obvious that it will be essential, at this stage, to know how interested in specific schemes any potential developers may be. Some alternatives may depend more than others on the private market contribution, and this fact will be an important one when selecting the best alternative and objectives.

The choice of alternatives and the evaluation of the final draft is not solely the result of public participation exercises. It will be a combination of interdependent powers involved in the decision-making process—the planning team, the elected representatives and the public.

The planner's role in this part of the process is to make clear to the two other groups what are the advantages and disadvantages of the various alternatives. The American sociologist Mel Webber has summarised the test of any plan in his now classic three questions: Who pays? Who benefits? Who decides? (10)

There would be no problem if one interest group answered to all three questions, but this is never the case. The first two questions cannot really be separated from the setting of objectives, with which groups would already have been identified, or the attempts to measure to what extent the various proposals fulfil set objectives, or benefit a certain group, or approximate to certain desired standards. A number of techniques has been developed to deal with this part of the planning process, under the generic term 'cost-benefit analysis'. *Evaluation in the planning process* by N Lichfield, P Kettle and M Whitbread is recommended here. (11)

As to the third of M Webber's questions—who is to decide on the best course of action?—it is inevitably the elected representatives and/or those who control the resources who have the power and take the decisions. They will decide whether alternative I, which means losses for group A and gains for group B, is better or worse than alternative II, which reverses the gains and losses and in doing so, they may allow political preference to outweigh technical factors. Lichfield mentions that the planner does not necessarily know in advance what criteria the decision-takers will use to choose the final plan. Therefore, he should include among the alternatives at least some that do not seem to rank at all high in the evaluation, since they may have political advantages that outweigh their apparent disadvantages. (12) This comment contradicts the basic assumptions of the goal achievement planning process, by substituting for explicit and rationally deduced objectives others which are politically imposed. The technical evaluation is needed, in any case, to spell out the costs and benefits; and to make explicit what the community is giving up in order to obtain the benefits offered by the chosen plan. And public participation is needed to disclose the various groups' priorities. These, together with the technical evaluation, are then presented to the politicians. As G Benveniste says, 'Since all decisions on resource allocations have an impact on future outcomes, not specifying priorities looks like manipulation and secrecy. The experts ask the politicians to show their cards. If the politicians hesitate, they must be hiding something.' (13)

Eventually, the decisions taken have to be acted upon; this may sound self-evident, but is not inevitable. Bureaucratic interest may frustrate any action, or may even achieve a decision which will in fact mean inertia, so that no action will follow. This has become particularly significant during the depression in the mid-1970s; in many authorities where there is a no-growth situation, the planner's role has become more that of an entre-preneur, promoting development and ensuring that things happen. In that sense, development is accepted as being for the public good, and the doubts about who gains and who loses are forgotten.

More generally, it may be remarked that published plans or reports to committees do not show how the decisions were taken, though they usually indicate what the choices were. Only by reading minutes of meetings (and especially between the lines) can the decision-making process be followed and, possibly, be understood.

# REFERENCES

1 Research has resulted in land use allocation models of a high degree of sophistication. See for instance the work done at the University of Cambridge, Land Use and Built Form Studies: Development of a Model of a Town, Working Paper Aug 26, 1969; and A Disaggregated Model of Urban Spatial Structure: Theoretical Framework, Working Paper 8, 1973.

2 Department of the Environment, Local Plans Note 1/76, Development Plan Scheme and Local Plans, Section 8.

3 R Hambleton, 'Local planning and area management', in *The planner*, vol 62, no 6, Sept 1976, p176.

4 DOE Local Plans Note 1/78, Form and Content of Local Plans, para 25, p7 and para 17, p5.

5 Chichester District Council, Manhood Local Plan, Alternatives Report, February 1976, part 3, para 1.1.

6 J K Friend and N Jessop, *Local government and strategic choice*, Tavistock, 1969. Notts-Derby Study Team, The Nottingham and Derbyshire Sub-regional Study, Nottingham County Council, 1969.

7 Barnsley Metropolitan Borough Council, Barnsley Town Centre Draft Action Area Plan, chapter 3, para 3.12, p 67.

8 Town & Country Planning (Structure and Local Plans) Regulations 1974, Schedule 2, part I and Reg 16 (1).

9 T MacMurray, 'Strengthening our approach', in *The planner*, vol 60, no 1, Jan 1974, p494.

10 M M Webber, 'Planning in an environment of change', part I 'Beyond the industrial age', in *Town planning review*, vol 39, 1969, pp194-195.

11 N Lichfield, P Keith and M Whitbread, *Evaluation in the planning process*, Pergamon Press, 1975. See also M Hill, 'A goals achievement matrix for evaluating alternative plans', in *Journal of the American Institute of Planners*, no 34, 1968, p19.

12 N Lichfield, op cit, para 3.2, p41.

13 G Benveniste, *The politics of expertise*, The Glendessary Press, Berkeley, California, 1972, p70.

Chapter 6

# IMPLEMENTATION AND THE FORM OF THE PLAN

To implement means 'to carry into effect' and this, in the short term at least, is what planning should be about. For a plan, be it approved by all the authorities in the realm, is nothing but a series of paper documents. Implementation, moreover, is the only essential part of the planning process, the point where theories and policies become realities. It occurs regardless of the existence or absence of a 'plan'; and the plan can only be as good as its implemented realisation. A prospectively excellent plan can fail miserably because of bad management during its implementation. Additionally, the way the plan is prepared, and the form of the final document, can substantially help or hinder its implementation. This chapter looks at some of the important elements of the implementation process—and where they sometimes fail. The three issues are 'management', 'control and stimulation', and 'monitoring'. They occur simultaneously and in parallel, and only for the purpose of analysis are they considered separately here.

## Management
Local government has become very management-conscious in the past few years. It has adopted new techniques with the purpose of making its work more effective. In planning, 'planning programming and budgeting systems' and 'critical path analysis' are two examples widely covered by the available literature, which need not be re-examined here. (1)

But, good management is more than a chart on the wall, or an elaborate diagram composed of boxes and arrows. Management is defined as 'skilful handling', something for which local government officers are not always trained. It requires, in our context, a commitment to the success of the plan, a confidence in the validity of the policies, and the trust of the public in the planners. B McLoughlin has pointed out the importance of development control officers' know-how in dealing with people: 'The essential ability is dealing with people in face-to-face situations, the ability to be helpful in guiding them through the labyrinths of officialdom.' (2) This quality seems essential not only for a development control officer but for anyone involved in the implementation of a plan.

Some of the commonest failures are the ones that the general public notices most, delays, lack of coordination and confusing information are the most usual. Once a plan has been publicised and approved, delay in starting the authorities' proposed developments can turn the public's mind against any scheme. Delay may have been acceptable during the earlier stages of the process and, indeed, quite justified by the need to involve the public or to get further information, but it cannot be accepted during implementation. Similarly, lack of coordination within a department, or between departments, will create irritating and confusing situations, which antagonises the public and the developers. In 1974, at a conference on housing organised by the TCPA, Susan Howard gave an example of this kind of situation when she referred to a scheme where traffic management was to be combined with environmental improvements: 'The confusion was compounded by the fact that the pavement extensions were built on one-way streets before any signs were erected telling people that it was a one-way street. We therefore had the unedifying spectacle of traffic going in both directions along a street which was no longer wide enough. In consequence, many motorists drove over the extensions causing considerable damage.' (3)

Islington provides a more fundamental instance. During 1973 and 1974, Islington Borough Council bought a very large number of tenanted properties, in some cases whole estates of about 500 dwellings. The houses had been poorly maintained and the residents were welcoming the possibility of becoming council tenants and having their dwellings improved. However, because of the large numbers involved and the lack of financial resources, the improvements are taking a long time to materialise. The tenants are disaffected and the council incurs the risk of being labelled a slum landlord. The same problems may arise with equal force from straightforward absence of communication or appropriate channels for the transfer of information between interested parties.

In order to avoid these pitfalls, the team implementing the plan should, like managers in industry, not only have technical skills, but also know how to negotiate, how to sell, how to deal with people. Additionally, there should be continuity between the preparation and the implementation stages. Unfortunately, too often planning departments are divided into a 'planning section' (under such names as 'research and intelligence' or 'development plan unit') and a 'control section'. One deals with preparing the plan up to its approval; the second takes over from there, having had no say in the plan's conception and, therefore, having little feeling of involvement with it. Similarly, it is rarely the planning department alone which will be affected and involved in the implementation of a plan. Other departments concerned should also take part in the preparation stages if they are going to have to implement it. Therefore, instead of the ridiculous situation of one group preparing the plan and handing it down to another group to put into practice, the team responsible for the plan

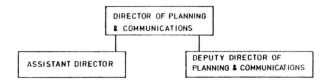

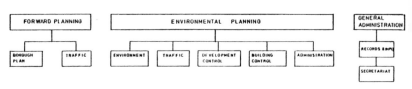

Fig 11: The organisation of a planning department: Camden Borough Council.
Notice the division between various sections and their names.

all the way should include members of all departments involved and,
ideally, be located in the area being dealt with. It should have wide
powers to deal with all aspects of the plan's implementation, and be
directly responsible to an area committee—which might include local
representatives and, certainly, should include the local ward's councillors.
In an article in *Built environment* D Gransby summed up the situation:
'In negotiations with the planning authority a developer can be faced with
as many as fourteen different departments by no means speaking in
unison. It would certainly improve the system if team leaders could act
in general coordinative capacity, or if a general planning team to vet all
major schemes across the board could be set-up, rather than the present
round-robin situation of interdepartmental referrals, which waste public
and private time and money.' (4)

### Control and stimulation
At present, the most time-consuming part of the planning process is
probably the control of development.

The post-1968 legislation is intended to ensure that this control trans-
mutes proposals into realities. (5) The abundant literature on the subject
and the discussions that have taken place in the last few years, indicate
the lack of satisfaction with the present system: the Dobry Report, the
review of the General Development Order by the DOE and the DOE's
78

Report on the Value of Standards for the External Residential Environment, to mention but a few. (6)

What has been said about management obviously applies here as well; but, additionally, certain tools exist which need considering within the new framework. Great emphasis is laid in the *Development plan manual* on two apparently conflicting terms, detailed information and flexibility: 'Though the aim will be to give a maximum of freedom to the designers, there will be a need to state the aspects which the authority regard as essential to the proper development of the area.' (7)

Although no clear indication is given of how this is to be achieved in practice, it seems that traditional measures of development control will not be successful and that new ways will have to be found to ensure that development of the type and quality desired takes place. Failures seem most obvious when design aspects are considered, but the application of control criteria to other issues has not been much more successful. Land-use zoning and planning standards, such as residential density, plot ratio and parking standards, are the more usual controls applied. In general terms, they will have disappeared from the structure plans, at least in their traditional form. But will they reappear in local plans?

Zoning, as applied in the past, seems at the same time too general, too crude and too rigid. It does not encourage combining uses on one site; it does not guarantee that a proposal on paper will become a reality; and it creates an absurd situation when a large number of activities are labelled as 'non-conforming', because for some years they do not match the plan. When dealing with a local area, the planning team may have identified certain needs, a number of activities that should be encouraged to come to or remain in the area. There may be a quantification of acceptable uses of land, that are expected to exist in the area as a whole for it to function in accordance with policy objectives. These would relate to the existing situation and the direction of change which appears most likely, and as and when the situation changes, they would also be modified. For key sites, where changes are of strategic importance and/or imminent, detailed briefs would be prepared after discussions with the developer. These briefs would specify exactly the uses, their quantities and disposition—not simply 'shop use, residential and commercial', say, but 'shops of such kind and size, dwellings for a particular kind of household and offices of a specific kind and size.'

Considerations such as the economic viability or the social desirability of the proposed uses would be taken into account; not physical elements exclusively, nor blanket concepts of residential and industrial uses. Although the DOE has emphasised that local plans are land-use plans, and should not deal with aspects which do not fall directly under the town and country planning legislation, the department has accepted that they are not zoning maps: 'The proposals map is not a zoning map showing how all the land in the area it covers is proposed to be used. . . In the absence of any proposal in the local or structure plan relating to the land in respect of which an application for planning permission is made, there will be no presumption either for or against the particular development.' (8)

The use of residential densities seems equally unsatisfactory as a control tool. It does not ensure that buildings will be used in the way plans indicate they should be, and it gives a false impression of precision. Even in local authority housing schemes, where there is a high level of control over occupancy, density levels tend to fall sharply after a few years of occupation. Conversely, in privately rented accommodation, the level of occupation may push densities far above the standard established. Related to this is the fact that net residential densities only partly indicate the need for services, facilities and other uses related to the life of the residents—which is another excuse for using them as a standard. For instance, two areas built at 100 persons per acre may have populations of completely different age structures, needing very different kinds of services— say, a primary school in one case and a geriatric clinic in the other.

Additionally, environmental standards, which densities are supposed to enforce, are either subject to other kinds of controls as well, such as daylighting, open space, noise, pollution, overlooking, etc; or are not really controlled by density measures—such as aesthetic aspects, landscaping, height of buildings, etc. Finally, density controls are sometimes used for totally different purposes from the ones they are intended for—to protect the socio-economic status of an area, to discourage certain kinds of development, or as a protection against poor design.

To conclude this critique of the use of density for control purposes, a few quotes from the DOE's Research Report no 6 on the Value of Standards for Residential Development, are relevant here: 'A density standard is a lazy form of design control, an unsatisfactory short cut which tends to perpetuate traditional forms of design and does not make allowances for the provision that ought to be made in particular circumstances.' 'There is, however, something unsatisfactory in using failure to comply with standards as a formula of refusal, when the wider design reasons for refusal, which may be a great deal more justified, are not brought into the open.' 'Density standards directed at purely housing environment aims are so poorly related to these aims that they should be dropped in favour of more direct and effective ways of achieving them.' (9)

The answer to this kind of failure by a standard lies in the formulation of the plan. If the environment does not behave as the plan suggested, it is the plan which needs adjusting, not the environment! In the case of local areas, it should be possible to estimate, for a limited period of time ahead, the population potential and capacity of an area as a whole. The plan could, therefore, specify a range of population figures acceptable for the good functioning of the area and fulfilling certain policy objectives

80

A wide range of densities could be given to avoid excesses in both directions—over and under use of land. As was suggested with zoning, key sites may be earmarked for certain kinds of developments, where not only the total number of people would be indicated, but also the kinds of household and possibly the tenure, the socio-economic groups, etc. Outside these sites, and providing the total figures for the whole area were respected, the controls applied would be environmental, such as daylighting, height of buildings, spaces between them, etc.

Planners have at present a number of other tools with which to control development—plot-ratios, parking standards, use-classes, daylighting, etc. Some of these are standardised and uniformly applied throughout the country, others are more or less 'ad hoc' measures taken by individual authorities. A number of these will be incorporated in local plans, although some may not come directly under planning legislation. In the case of standards such as plot-ratios or other measures of commercial density, it is suggested that a similar flexibility to that applied for residential areas is appropriate—detailed briefs for key sites and wide ranges for the rest of the area, with the proviso that the objectives for the area must be fulfilled and other standards safeguarded.

Specific policies referring to issues particularly relevant to a local authority, or a particular area, may also become part of the local plan or, in some cases, constitute a subject plan. Among them are, for instance, the 'small dwelling policies' operated by inner London boroughs at one time, fixing a limit to the number or proportion of one- and two-person dwellings that can be included in any one residential development. (10)

finally, there are the design and aesthetic controls. Development control officers often remark on the fact that these are the aspects on which most time is spent when reviewing an application and negotiating with developers. In spite of this, the results are too often unsatisfactory, and criticisms of the planning system by the general public tend to focus on visual and environmental aspects. Here it is sufficient to give as an example the approach taken by Essex County Council in its *Design guide for residential areas*. The foreword contains the following comment by the then Secretary of State, Geoffrey Rippon, which seems to summarise a large number of planning problems, but is particularly relevant to such imponderable factors as aesthetics: 'While much can be done to improve the quality of development through the statutory process of planning control, this can be a source of friction and wasteful of time and scarce resources if there is a lack of understanding between the public and the planners.' (11)

All this having been said, any form of control will be of little practical value if no applications are forthcoming as a result, or if potential developers withdraw their interest because of planning requirements. The role of the local authority must include stimulation of the non-public

81

sector. Peter Headicar, writing about planning authorities dealing with town centres, said: 'First, they must create those features in the plan (for example, highways or car parks) which they themselves have planned. Second, they must influence the activities of the private sector so that developments of the kind indicated in the plan materialise in the time and place specified.' (12)

This will be achieved through negotiations conducted throughout the planning process, by providing incentives, by including the kind of uses which will attract investment, etc. Particularly in recent years, planners have had to become much more involved in the promotion of development at a time when economic growth is seen as an overriding objective.

An additional point needs to be made. Planners often complain of the weakness of their powers to impose standards on private sector activities. While this may well be true, local authority and other public bodies' own schemes have rarely in the past achieved aesthetic standards higher than the private ones, the DOE building in Marsham Street is probably one of the most glaring examples. Powers of control should be stronger, and they should apply to all applicants in the same way.

A quotation from the already mentioned DOE Research Report no 6 is appropriate to close this section: 'It seems that the importance attached to standards in general and to certain standards in particular may also depend on thoughtless habit: densities, road widths, and in some places privacy distances may have been applied for so long that they are taken completely for granted. Standards which are new, especially if they present technical difficulties, may be less used, not from lack of conviction but because time to master and apply them would have to be fitted in to a heavy day of routine work.' (13)

## Monitoring

It is a platitude to observe that the process of planning does not end with the publication of 'the plan'. It is a continuously evolving process, and policies should constantly be revised and, where necessary, modified during implementation. Much has been said about the need for flexibility, but this is not of itself sufficient; a way of discovering early enough what changes in the environment require adaptation of the plan is equally important. Often, planning policies arrive too late because the symptoms of change have not been discovered in time. As mentioned before, close communication between development plan and development control officers is one way of improving the sensitivity to change. The results of planning applications or of enquiries should continuously be fed back into the process. Several local authorities have already developed such a system, with weekly meetings between development control and development planning officers, to review all enquiries and applications in a particular area. Integrated area teams, as already mentioned, would be a further improvement on this.

82

Since, it is to be hoped, the plans will not just be physical ones, monitoring should go beyond land-use policies and incorporate all aspects of local government and private activity affecting the local area. Therefore, a fairly elaborate information system must be established, to include all departments and organisations concerned, on the lines proposed by the DOE's Report on General Information Systems for Planners. (14)

The feed-back should induce reconsideration of the plan at all levels— objectives, policies and actions. It may be that the original objectives have not changed, but that the plan is not achieving them, either because the policies are wrong or because, although the policies are right, they are not put into practice through the right actions. Alternatively, the objectives may be being achieved but no longer be valid. Readjustments of the whole system should, therefore, occur constantly.

Finally, monitoring should go beyond the local plan itself, and information should be fed back into the structure plan to help to modify it as well as and when necessary. With the present division of responsibilities and the often reluctant collaboration between districts and counties, this may be difficult to achieve; but it is essential if the process is to retain its validity over a period of time. 'Some authorities are now beginning to bring development control and development plan work more closely together, to counteract the isolation (and also the comparative unpopularity) of development control work. In future, development controllers may also have to work in a more integral way with personnel outside the planning department.' (15)

### The form of the plan
The way planning is to be implemented affects the form in which the planning document is presented. What sort of document will fit the suggestions of the previous pages, which have implied what it will *not* be—ie a zoning, land-use map with blanket densities, plot-ratios, etc. But to indicate what is to replace this, is another matter. The document will be directed to three groups of interested parties:

a) The local authority, for which it will be a decision-making tool in relation to its own investments and the control of private action.

b) The general public, for whom it will be an information and discussion document.

c) The developers, for whom it will be a guide and a brief.

The document should serve to test the effect of certain proposed actions and/or suggest what further actions will be needed to move in a particular direction, and it should be an instrument to encourage dialogue between the various groups involved—an operational model and a basis for discussion. In this sense it is perhaps more a record of a process than a plan designed in the traditional form. It indicates the present state of affairs, the elements thereof which should be retained, and the new elements that it is of fundamental importance to introduce. In the case of Action Areas, there should be new developments, private or public, for which detailed briefs are included in the document, together with the designation of the acting agency. Policies of the kind, 'If A happens, then B should happen'; or 'If A, then B or C', and general guidelines, should also be included. Otherwise, where predictions about the future can be little more than reasoned guesses, flexibility should be allowed, and only indications of objectives, opportunities, ranges of possibilities and performance criteria should be made explicit.

The *Development plan manual* is fairly non-committal about its requirements: 'All local plans will consist of a map together with other diagrams and illustrations where necessary and a written statement. In addition, authorities may wish to set out and publish a fuller technical justification for their proposals than is possible in the written statement.' In comparing the proposals map to the old style development plan, it states: 'Firstly it does not aim to give a comprehensive picture of all land-uses at some date in the future, but defines only those sites where the authority is committed to change of a specified nature; and secondly it identifies the areas within which specific development control policies are to operate.' (16)

The manual does go on to suggest items which have to be included in the written statement—a description of the area, an outline of structure plan policies as they affect the area, the relationship with other local plans, the outline of policies and proposals, their phasing and their implementation. Guidance to private developers should be 'selective' but should include 'matters not open to negotiation'. Unfortunately, net residential density is one example given of the latter! (17)

From the various examples analysed, it seems that most authorities have accepted these instructions in general terms and adapted them to their particular need. Maps vary from the almost incomprehensible diagram of the Camden borough plan to detailed coloured maps such as those for Richmond town centre and Eden Street Action Area. Some maps are only coloured to indicate proposed changes in the land-use; others have the existing new uses included; and some have other policies added, varying from conservation to industrial relocation, from traffic management schemes to GIA proposals. The written statements differ in content and form depending on the approach taken and the scope of the plan. Examples and quotations throughout this book provide a fair idea of the variety.

More recently, and having had the opportunity of inspecting a number of local plans, the DOE has given an indication of what it expects to see in a submitted plan. This has been summarised in Note 1/78. From the formal point of view, local plans should, as before, consist of a written statement setting out the proposals and their reasoned justification, and a

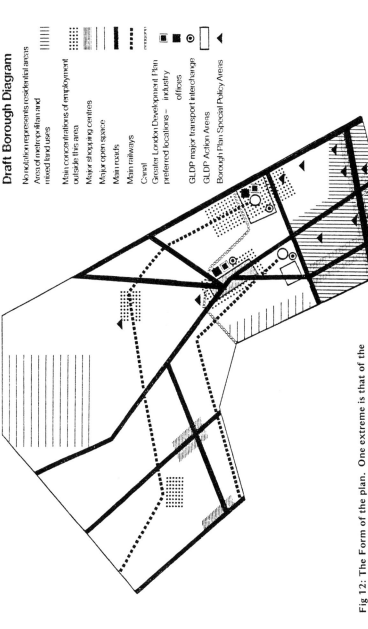

## Draft Borough Diagram

No notation represents residential areas

Area of metropolitan and mixed land uses

Main concentrations of employment outside this area

Major shopping centres

Major open space

Main roads

Main railways

Canal

Greater London Development Plan preferred locations – industry
offices

GLDP major transport interchange

GLDP Action Areas

Borough Plan Special Policy Areas

**Fig 12: The Form of the plan. One extreme is that of the Camden diagram. (This has not been used in the final document published by Camden Borough Council.)**

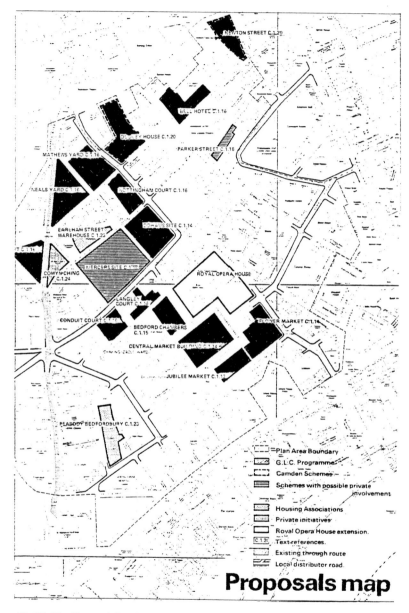

NEWTON STREET C.1.20

BELL HOTEL C.1.16

DUDLEY HOUSE C.1.20

PARKER STREET C.1.18

MATHEWS YARD C.1.16

NEALS YARD C.1.16

NOTTINGHAM COURT C.1.16

EARLHAM STREET WAREHOUSE C.1.23

ODHAMS SITE C.1.14

C.1.16

MERCERS SITE C.1.17

COMYN CHING C.1.24

ROYAL OPERA HOUSE

LANGLEY COURT C.1.16

CONDUIT COURT C.1.16

BEDFORD CHAMBERS C.1.15

FLOWER MARKET C.1.14

CENTRAL MARKET BUILDING C.1.14 C.

CHARING CROSS ROAD

JUBILEE MARKET C.1.14

PEABODY BEDFORDBURY C.1.23

Plan Area Boundary
G.L.C. Programme
Camden Schemes
Schemes with possible private involvement
Housing Associations
Private initiatives
Royal Opera House extension.
C.1.2( Text-references.
Existing through route
Local distributor road.

## Proposals map

Fig 13: The Form of the plan. Another example: Covent Garden proposals map.
Source: Greater London Council, Covent Garden Action Area Plan.

86

proposals map. The proposals must relate to development and other use of land, and they should be distinguished from the rest of the text by a different style of type. If a local authority has, as has been recommended in this book, treated an area comprehensively and dealt with all aspects of local government involvement, it should not include non-town-planning policies (HAA's or GIA's for example) as part of the plan's policies, though they can be referred to in the reasoned justification. Four important reasons for this are given in the note: 'First to make clear to the public which parts of the plan have statutory force following adoption; secondly to ensure that the plan is not unnecessarily affected by the termination or alteration of the related non-planning activities (ie so that development control has a sound basis even if, say, an HAA is terminated); thirdly to help the local planning authority bring forward full and sustainable expressions of their proposals for the development or other use of land; and fourthly to avoid confusion with procedures laid down by Parliament under different statutes.' (18)

Only the second reason seems to have something beyond bureaucratic value; in terms of the general public and their involvement in the planning process, it is foolish to expect a neat division of local authorities' responsibilities, as is suggested in the Note.

The report of survey can be put on deposit with the written statement and the proposals map, but is not seen as part of the plan. The proposals map 'should define only those areas where the designated planning authority makes proposals (including those of other agencies) for specific developments or other uses of land or the operation of specified policies.'

Diagrams like the one in Camden's plan are frowned upon because of their imprecise character and the possibilities of confusion: 'An imprecise intention should not be distinguished as a proposal in the written statement or shown on the proposals map. (19)

## REFERENCES

1   See for instance J Welfare, 'Programme budgeting, the experience at Milton Keynes' in the *Journal of the Royal Town Planning Institute*, vol 57, no 8, Sept/Oct 1971, p361. For an introduction to PPBS, see F J Lyden and E G Miller, *Planning programming budgeting*, Markham Publishing Co, Chicago, 1972. For critical path analysis, see K G Lockyer, *An introduction to critical path analysis*, Pitman, London, 1964, and *Critical path analysis: problems and solutions*, Pitman, London, 1969.

2   J B McLoughlin, 'A future for development control', in *Proceedings of Seminar M, Development Control and Plan Implementation*, PTRC Summer Annual Meeting, July 1974, p99.

3  S Howard, 'An illustration of some of the practical difficulties in GIA's'. Paper delivered to the Town & Country Planning Association Conference on Housing in June 1974.

4  D Gransby, 'The malaise of delay', in *Built environment*, Dec 1973, p626.

5  See the Ministry of Housing and Local Government's Report of the Planning Advisory Group, *The future of development plans*, HMSO, 1965, chapter 1.

6  G Dobry, 'Review of the development control system', Report to the DOE, HMSO, 1975. The latest amendment to the GDO is the Town & Country Planning General Development Order 1977. DOE Research Report No 6, 'The value of standards for the external residential environment'. Report prepared by Woodford, Williams and Hill, 1976.

7  MOHLG, Development Plans—A Manual of Form and Content, HMSO, 1970, chapter 7, para 7.15, p43.

8  DOE Local Plans Note 1/78, Form and Content of Local Plans, para 39, p10.

9  DOE Research Report No 6, op cit, chapter 5, para 5.13, p40; chapter 4, para 4.19, p32 and chapter 5, Conclusions 1, p42.

10  For example, the London Borough of Islington applied a policy inherited from the London County Council, limiting the proportion of one- and two-room dwellings to a third of the total number of dwellings in any particular development.

11  Essex County Council, 'A design guide for residential areas', Dec 1973.

12  P Headicar, 'Town centre planning: a new style', in *The planner*, vol 60, no 8, Oct 1974, pp835-838.

13  DOE Research Report No 6, op cit, chapter 1, para 1.57, p19.

14  DOE and Scottish Development Department, Joint Local Authority Study Team, General Information System for Planning, HMSO, 1972. See also DOE, Research Report 1, General Review of Local Authority Management Information Systems, HMSO, 1975.

15  DOE Research Report no 6, op cit, chapter 4, para 4.9, p31.

16  MOHLG, Development Plans, op cit, chapter 7, p44, paras 7.17 and 7.18.

17  MOHLG, Development Plans, op cit, chapter 7, p45, para 7.26.

18  DOE Local Plans Note 1/78, Form and Content of Local Plans, para 17, p5.

19  DOE Local Plans Note 1/78, para 34, p8 and para 37, p9.

Chapter 7

# THE PROCESS OF DEVELOPMENT

Previous chapters have outlined the main parts of the planning process as applied on a local scale and the last one emphasised that implementation cannot, by definition, be divorced from the process of development.

Once the local plan has been adopted by the local authority and been given adequate publicity, most of the initiative thereafter is likely to come from the private sector. Interested developers will be recipients of the document, and will use it as one of the elements by which to evaluate the feasibility of developments they may want to undertake. The main purpose of this chapter is to introduce the chief participants in this process, and some of the situations that may commonly arise between developers and local planners.

Planners in the past have tended to leave financial considerations out of their analyses. Many a report to committee is prepared in the planning department and only then sent to the finance department for a brief paragraph to be inserted about financial implications. In the last few years, however, the economic situation has forced planners to be more conscious of development costs and how these may affect proposals. For without economic realism there is very little chance for positive planning to reach fulfilment; proposals only become realities if resources exist to implement them. Yet a review of a number of local plans still shows a depressing ignorance of the importance of these issues. For example, the Richmond town centre plan allocates one third of a page out of its 120 pages to financial considerations, and Windsor town centre draft plan ignores them altogether. (1)

The potential of the Community Land Act 1975 should force the planning profession to take costs into account, for local authorities may now become involved in commercial development, and planning matters thus have to be considered in a different light. (2) Local plans are to be the main instruments for programming land acquisition. It is too early to evaluate how this will affect the planning machinery or make for more successful planning. The success of the legislation will partly depend on the willingness of the local authorities to implement it for the benefit of the community as a whole, and not for short-term political gain or financial expediency.

## The actors in the development process

The purpose of the development process is to build upon and/or change the use of a parcel of land. In order to achieve this, the actors in the process perform a variety of roles. The provision of the land, its assembly, the control of the development, the building, the financing, the sale or management of the finished product, are all performed by individuals or agencies with specific skills and interests. Additionally, central government plays an important role through economic measures—taxation, control of interest rates, legislation, planning decisions, etc.

Land is the main resource that cannot be substituted, and one of the first stages of the process will be its assembly by the agency which wants to undertake the development. The developer will begin a search of the market, via contact with estate agents and landowners with a view to acquiring land—which may or may not be readily available. Landowners may not wish to sell, or may be themselves developers who want to keep a stock to ensure the continuity of their own operations; and both may be motivated by speculative reasons. Alternatively, it can be the local authority's development plan or the lack of a services infrastructure which restrict the release of land for particular uses.

The developer's motivation is economic—the maximisation of profit—whether he is a holding company, using existing investment in property assets to raise loans for further investments, or a trading company dealing in property as a commodity. Exceptionally, the development may be undertaken by the local authority itself, or by another public agency, with a different kind of motivation from that of the private sector—the achievement of societal goals. In most cases, however, the purchase of land is a market-economy operation, influenced by supply and demand.

The decision to buy is a fundamental one since upon it hinges the whole development process, and its price is the ultimate determinant of the decision. The price the developer is prepared to pay depends on the site, the planning constraints, the cost of the development, the market demand for that particular kind of development, and on possible agreements with the landowner such as to buy only part of the desired land at first, with options on the rest. The calculations made by the developer can be summarised by the following equation:

$$P - C = R$$

where P is the capitalised market price or market value of the completed development, C its total cost of implementation (including interest payable on the money employed or borrowed and the profit plus a safety margin against adverse circumstances), R is the residual—the maximum price to pay for the land if the development is to be financially viable.

The local authority's role in the process, through development plans, is to let the developer know what the potential of an area is, what constraints affect a particular site, and what kind of development might be encouraged. Its policies will also affect the demand for a particular use, or displace it from one area to another. In principle, the role of the planner should be to make land available for the kind of use desired, in the right place and at the right time, in order to achieve stipulated social goals. Through development control, local authorities have veto powers over most kinds of proposal, and the veto is their main instrument by which they eventually achieve their policy aims. Additionally, they can acquire land for development, by agreement with a landowner or, if necessary, through compulsory purchase powers (which have to be confirmed by central government). In spite of their powers, public authorities have only exceptionally—as in the case of the new towns—succeeded in controlling the release of land and coordinating development. For that reason, the Community Land Act was given the Royal Assent in 1975. The related White Paper, 'Land', stated the purpose of the legislation as being:

'a) to enable the community to control the development of land in accordance with its needs and priorities; and

b) to restore to the community the increase in value of land arising from its efforts.' (3)

All the various agencies—landowners, developers, financial institutions providing loan capital and local authorities—interact in the development process, and have their own interests in mind. Major conflicts can arise between the public interest as represented by planning needs and the profit criteria of the private market. The situation is complicated by the duality of certain agencies—British Railways acting as a developer, a trade union's pension fund as a financier, and a local authority as a landowner/developer. Planning authorities do not possess the resources to achieve their goals without the collaboration of the private market; and, conversely, the purposes of the market place may sometimes be frustrated by the local authorities' decisions. (4)

Nowhere do these conflicts appear more clearly than in local planning. The functions of local plans were outlined earlier in the book; the basic intention of the legislation was to provide a more positive role for the planning authorities. In absolute terms this is an impossible requirement unless they become developers or work hand-in-hand with them; and there is a basic contradiction between expecting local plans to interpret the macro-strategies handed down from the structure plans, and at the same time give a positive impulse to local market forces, which vary at a much quicker pace than can be predicted in long-term planning.

In our (far from ideal) mixed economy, social goals and private profits are generally not similar, but they are not necessarily incompatible either. During the late sixties and early seventies, the main emphasis was on the differences; the planners and the developers were increasingly suspicious of the actions and motivations of each other.

In broad terms, the private sector trains people to be skilled managers with a flair for financially successful land deals and development opportunities. Property companies employ people whose expertise includes the knowledge of how to get around the planners and get the most advantageous deal from the local authorities. They consider that the latter impose additional and unnecessary costs upon the development through delays and requirements that reduce the profitability of the schemes. The debates that followed the Dobry report on development control often centred on the economic waste that resulted from planning controls. Additionally, developers feel their antagonism justified when a decision first held against them is then reversed on appeal. An example of this is given by the investigation and report on Islington borough council's planning department by C Price (5)

However, on the other side of the fence, planners are part of the bureaucratic machinery, and as such they respond to political pressures and are rarely able to take initiatives of their own except perhaps in relation to local authorities' own development. In his book *Land policy*, John Ratcliffe pointed out that the planner's role is not necessarily negative, but it is passive. (6)

### Planning gains

For a number of years, local authorities have inclined to the view that private developers were 'getting away with murder', making huge profits without the community receiving any share of benefits, or the planners being able to influence them. In parallel, lack of funds and of control of land made it difficult for authorities to provide social amenities, often non-essential but desirable, particularly in those areas where developers activities resulted in high land values. Some planning authorities have, therefore, instituted a practice of negotiating with developers seeking planning permission for commercial development, with the purpose of persuading them partly to repay the community via the provision of public buildings or services, the restoration of an historic building or, more often, the provision of council housing. The nature and magnitude of this so called 'planning gain' (7) has varied substantially from case to case, but it is certain that the developer's profit has not been destroyed by his contribution to the common good, but in some cases, has actually been increased. A shopping centre development was granted permission to proceed and the developer entered into an agreement with the local authority to provide a bus terminal on part of the site. Public use of the terminal had the effect of attracting more customers than expected to the centre, and the developers were able to charge higher rents than might have been the case if the 'planning gain' had not materialised.

Under section 52 of the Town & Country Planning Act 1971, local authorities are able to enter into these agreements, covered by covenants, with landowners regarding the use and development of their land, prior to granting planning permission. (8) Although these powers, which existed already under the 1962 Act, have been used, their scope is limited by their voluntary character, and by the difficulty of enforcing them against successors of the developer with whom the agreement has been reached. However, since 1974, local authorities can in certain cases use Housing Act powers to enforce positive covenants against third parties, and General Powers Acts can be used for the same purpose. (9)

The main problem with planning gains is their unpredictable character. The initiative lies with the developer; only when the planning application is first raised can negotiations start, and each side will try to get the maximum out of the other. The developer, knowing that he will have his potential profits under attack, but not knowing to what extent and in what way, may start by offering a scheme more ambitious than he really intends to create. Or, on the other hand, the local authority may not have any particular project in mind, but will invent one just to get something out of the developer, even if it is not a real gain, and may try to impose conditions which are 'ultra vires' and impossible to enforce legally.

Again, local planning may help in making a positive asset out of the concept of planning gains. The local authorities may set out in their local plans what they expect to get as trade-offs on specific sites: housing in a shopping centre, a public square in front of an office building, a particular community use in a commercial development. Draft briefs of this sort can be prepared in advance of the developer's application and included in the local plan, where it is known that potential exists.

### Partnership schemes

One step further in local authority involvement in the development process is shown by the various experiments in partnership which have occured between the public and private sectors. Traditionally, local authorities have mainly been involved in housing development. But they are owners of large tracts of land and they can undertake, either on their own or in some form of partnership, developments of other kinds. The arrangements have varied from granting a lease on land with infrastructure and a specific development brief, to forming a development partnership for a specific purpose. Buckinghamshire county, Norwich district and Hampshire county are examples of authorities which have embarked on partnership schemes. (10)

The rationale of and the motivation towards these schemes are easily perceived: the local authority can control the development much more closely, recover part of the 'profit' for the community, obtain a contribution towards the cost of infrastructure, and raise finance outside central government control. The developer gets land, part of which he may not have had to pay for, compulsory purchase help for land assembly, planning permission and an asset he can subsequently sell. For both sides, the main advantage stems from the fact that the development actually takes place.

A few examples will illustrate the kinds of partnership that have been tried. Buckinghamshire county and the Aylesbury Vale district council acquired shares in a private company to buy land for housing development. The land was bought cheaply, sold to the developer at a profit and part of this latter was used to pay for the infrastructure. In another case, Norwich district council entered into partnership with a developer to acquire land which had seemed unattractive to the private market and developed it for a mixture of uses, some for profit and some socially orientated. Manchester district council formed a limited company to finance private development in the city centre. Hampshire county council has an agreement with a merchant bank to assemble land on an option basis over ten years. The list is far from comprehensive and many other possibilities exist. As can be seen, the company does not necessarily buy the land or develop it, but it ensures that the development does take place. (11)

The disadvantages of these schemes lie in the commercial risks inherent in the operation and in conflicts of interests. Limited companies have to be commercially successful and are responsible to their shareholders; local authorities have social goals and are responsible to their ratepayers. However, there do exist sufficient statutory controls to ensure that desired and rational development can take place without involving ratepayers in financial loss. Planning at both structure and local level is one of these forms of control.

### The community land scheme
After thirty years of planning legislation and a number of failed attempts to deal with the problem of worsenment and betterment, two new Acts were passed by Parliament in 1975/76—the Community Land Act and the Development Land Tax Act. It is an indictment of the whole planning system that this new legislation is specifically intended to achieve more effective and positive planning—implying that in the past it has been neither. (12)

This is not the place to go into the contended evils of the legislation, and only a few elements of it need to be outlined here. The new Acts have been implemented in phases, starting with the First Appointed Date (FAD) on April 6 1976 in England and Wales, and the introduction of the Land Tax in August 1976. Only after the Second Appointed Date (SAD), yet to be fixed, will the system be fully operational. In the interim period, Development Land Tax is to be charged on 'realised development value' resulting from the sale of land, ie on the difference between market value and current use value. Authorities are able to acquire land at market value less any DLT; if they sell it subsequently, they can do so at market value,

94

therefore making a profit for the community. After the SAD, the basic elements of the scheme will be:

a) Land suitable for 'relevant' development will be acquired by local authorities at a price which excludes development value.

b) 'Relevant' development can only take place on land publicly owned or that has been through public ownership.

c) Private deals in land will be subject to a tax on the increase in value due to development or development potential. The rate of this tax will vary over time, and for the moment local authorities will not pay it.

Authorities have, therefore, the power to acquire land 'suitable for development' and, in certain cases, the duty to do so. There are various types of development—relevant, exempted and excepted—the definitions of which can be found in S3(2) of the Act, Sch1 of the Act and the Community Land (Excepted Development) Regulations 1976. (13)

The scheme does not require that local authorities develop all relevant land themselves. They can do so, or may dispose of it on a leasehold or freehold basis, depending on the use, the circumstances and the best interest of the community. It is, however, expected that, in general, housing land will be sold freehold and in other cases leasehold arrangements with periodic rent reviews will be made.

Parts of the legislation have yet to be explained and detailed by the DOE; and the Community Land Act is not yet fully in operation. It is, therefore, premature to assess its value and consequences. But from the large number of reactions to the Act, some comments can be selected which are relevant to local planning. The DOE has produced a booklet on the Community Land Scheme, entitled *An introduction*, in which it is stated: 'Where land is needed for housing, industry or commerce, authorities will have to plan to make this available, provided that this can be done within the planning policies for their area.' (14)

The proviso highlights a potential conflict in the spirit of the legislation. In theory, of course, planning policies should reflect land needs; but in practice, desired development (public profit) may not be in the best interest of positive community planning (public good).

The political thinking which led to the Act started at a time of economic expansion and of optimistic forecasts about the future of the development industry. Since then, the optimism has been reversed and local government affected by major cuts in spending power. If the supply of land for development dries up and few schemes are put forward, this will be blamed on the legislation—perhaps wrongly, for the recession may be the main cause. However, there is a basic contradiction in introducing legislation demanding investment and an expansion of the bureaucracy at the same time that the facts of economic life are in opposition to both.

It must be said that the institution of Development Land Tax is likely to seriously discourage the partnership schemes referred to in the previous

95

section since the private companies which are involved will be taxed whether their partner is a public authority or not. And as L Robinson and B Wates pointed out in *Planning* (September 1976), the tax may also see the end of planning gains arrangements, since developers will be taxed regardless of whether their scheme includes a socially desirable 'give away' element or not. (15)

Finally, in the town centres where land values are already very high, the community will not obtain any benefit from land transactions, yet it is often in these areas that relevant development ought to and does take place.

However, with all its potential faults, the Community Land Scheme should at least ensure that planners become more conscious of the importance of market forces if their plans are to become realities, and, in that sense, more positive planning should be achieved as a result. In particular, much more and better use is likely to be made of development briefs which the local authorities will prepare for sites where they wish to see particular forms of development. Professor Eddison has said: 'Development control policy and local plan policy should be interdependent. The case existed before community land. Now it is absolutely essential that the organisation and processes reflect this need, so that gradually one set of policies is developed from which speedy decisions about acquisition, disposal and planning consent can be based.' (16)

## REFERENCES

1   London Borough of Richmond upon Thames, Richmond Town Centre, Action Area Plan Report, February 1976. Royal Borough of Windsor and Maidenhead, Windsor Town Centre District Plan, August 1977.

2   The Community Land Act 1975, c77, HMSO.

3   Department of the Environment, Land (Cmnd 5730), Government White Paper, HMSO, 1975.

4   For further reading, see for instance: D Cadman and L Austin-Crowe, *Property development*, Spon, London, 1978. DOE, Report of the Working Party on Local Authority/Private Enterprise Partnership Schemes, HMSO, 1972. Advisory Group on Commercial Development, First report of the Advisory Group (The Pilcher Report), HMSO, 1975.

5   C Price, 'Islington and the Planning Acts, a critical enquiry, June 1975', CIP Development Securities Ltd and Nigel Moore and Associates.

6   J Ratcliffe, *Land policy*, Hutchinson, London, 1976, chapter 6, p84.

7   This widely used expression is a misnomer typical of planning jargon, which does not seem yet to have been accorded an official definition.
96

8  Town & Country Planning Act 1971, S52, which amends S37 of the Town & Country Planning Act 1962.

9  Housing Act 1971, c44, Part VII, S75. For a wider discussion of the section 52 agreements and other planning agreements, see R N D Hamilton, 'Drafting planning agreements' in *Local government chronicle*, Sept 16 1977, pp739-741, and J Jowell, 'Bargaining in development control', in *Journal of planning and environment law*, 1977, pp414-433.

10  See DOE, op cit, and J Thornley and R Minns, 'The Community Land Act and shareholding schemes', in *Local government chronicle*, Feb 1976, p169.

11  See also G Powell, 'Local authority participation in the profits of local property developments and the disposal of land by local authorities', in *Chartered surveyor: urban quarterly*, Feb 1974.

12  The Development Land Tax Act 1976, c24, HMSO.

13  For further explanations, see: G Parsons and B Redding, *Planning, development and the Community Land Scheme*, The Rating and Valuation Association, London, 1976; and The Boisont Waters Cohen Partnership, *The Community Land Act explained*, The Architectural Press, London, 1976.

14  DOE, *The Community Land Scheme'* Booklet 1, Introduction, HMSO, 1976.

15  L Robinson and B Waters, 'The land scheme and planning gain' in *Planning*, Sept 10 1976, p4.

16  Tony Eddison, 'The challenge of community land, 13, a final check list', in *Municipal and public services journal*, April 23, 1976, p479.


NOTE: At the time of going to press, the Conservative Government, elected in May 1979, has announced its intention to repeal the Community Land Act 1975 in the future.

Chapter 8

# DESIGN FACTORS

'The new system, with its more positive approach, will facilitate the creation of a good environment in both town and country.' (1)

'One of the objects of development control is to prevent bad design and encourage good. . . One cannot lay down rules defining what is good and what is bad, for aesthetic judgements are largely subjective and opinions, including expert opinions, often differ. . .' (2)

To achieve a pleasant environment has always been one of the main aims of planning and the above quotations emphasise this. However, after thirty years of planning control, it cannot be said that the achievements have been encouraging; indeed, the main criticism that the general public has against planning is the low aesthetic level of new developments. It is now hoped that the post-1968 planning system and the Community Land Act will be more effective—but will they? This chapter considers whether local planning will be able to raise the level of design and other related questions. Should design be controlled at all? What factors have to be taken into account when judging a design? Can there be objective criteria?

Definite answers to these are virtually impossible and it follows that the purpose of this chapter is not to analyse design, but to discuss its control. The distinction between the two is important, and one that has often been ignored, leading to confusion about what is the role of the planner. With the foundations of the profession rooted in the architectural tradition, planners have often been expected actually to design the environment, and, indeed, they have done so in many celebrated cases—Sir Frederic Gibberd's design of Harlow New Town is one example. However, in most situations nowadays, a planner is only involved in the regulation of other people's designs; and whilst he should have some knowledge of design elements, and understand the language of designers, he need not be a designer himself.

## Physical determinism
In the beginning was design . . . and, for a long time after, it remained design. The traditional approach to planning was based on the 'blue print'
98

concept—itself based on the assumption that if we design the right city (or environment), we shall obtain a good community. Principles applied to society were considered to work the same way as principles applied to physical aspects of the environment; therefore, it was assumed that predictions could be made about how society would behave in a number of years and that the proper environment could be designed for it. Because of the casual attitude of this approach, and its parallel with physical sciences, it was called 'physical determinism'. According to M Broady: 'It suggests that those human beings for whom architects and planners create their designs are simply moulded by the environment which is provided for them.' (3)

In the 1960's, and starting in the United States, this approach was challenged, and H Gans renamed it 'physical fallacy': 'The planners were enamoured of two environmental or physical fallacies: first, that the physical environment was a major determinant of society and culture; and second, that only an environment based on professional planning principles could deliver the good life.' (4)

In Britain, sociologists such as Broady attacked physical determinism in a similar way, and in a number of schools the training of town-planners moved away from an architectural approach to a discipline more related to the social sciences. It became fashionable to state that aesthetic or physical aspects had no effect on people and, by implication, that design was irrelevant.

However, within the writings of precisely those who attacked traditional approaches to planning, physical determinism crept back in a different form. Jane Jacobs did not suggest that planners should design 'beautiful' cities to achieve happy communities, but she did say that what people wanted was diversity and small scale development, and that, therefore, was what planners and architects should provide. (5) More recently, Oscar Newman suggested that one way of avoiding violence, crime and muggings was to design 'defensible spaces', and he supported his argument with a large number of analysed examples. (6)

Physical determinism is only one very general way of relating design to behaviour. Other concepts have been introduced and discussed by various authors, and they include the 'neighbourhood concept' widely used in new towns design; the territorial instinct of human beings; the process of learning about space (particularly in relation to children); the social effects of overcrowding, etc. These are the issues dealt with by the environmental psychologists, and a good review of them can be found in C Mercer's *Living in cities*. (7)

The argument continues, and I suggest that although Gans is right in condemning an approach to planning that bases people's satisfaction on the design of the environment but forgets basic needs such as shelter and employment, the attitude of ignoring completely the effect of physical

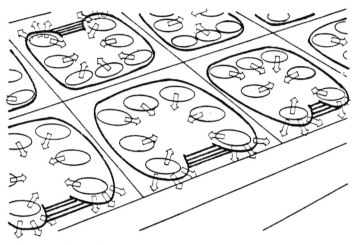

Schematic sketch illustrating territorial definition reinforced with surveillance opportunities (arrows).

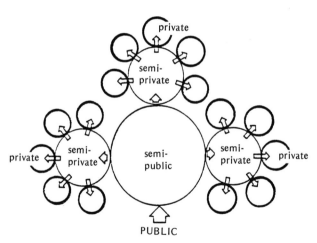

Schematic diagram illustrating evolving hierarchy of defensible space from public to private. Arrows indicate entries at different levels of the hierarchy.

Fig 14: Defensible Space, another form of physical determinism. Source: O. Newman, Defensible Space, Architectural Press, London, 1972.

100

aspects on people's lives is equally mistaken. In fact, people do react all the time to aesthetic elements in their environment: the majority of their comments (particularly critical ones) on the planners' achievements relate to these. The popular press often publishes comments about 'concrete jungles', drab environments, monotonous buildings, steel and glass monsters, boring developments, etc. Most of the time people have pointed out the negative aspects of the built environment and have related it to behaviour. Thus mental illness is related to tall buildings, marital problems and drug addiction to new towns. If the relationship exists in one direction, it must also exist in the other, more positive one. Social psychologists may explain that people are transferring their dislike of the system to an easier target, yet even though this may be true, the complaints remain.

Moreover, when people have a choice all other things being equal, they will prefer the better designed environment to the less good one. They will prefer A to B, will use C more often than D, remember E but forget F. A study might be made of pop songs dedicated to places: how many hearts have been left in San Francisco, how many in Detroit? There are always other explanations for these preferences but, when everything else has been considered, there remains an imponderable which relates to aesthetics. Gerald Burke, in his book *Townscapes*, summarises the relationship between people and their environment: 'Whilst it is fair to say that the interior of a building belongs to the client and must reflect his requirements, it is no less fair to say that the exterior belongs to the town and will have to be looked at by people for generations to come.' (8)

The scale on which people relate to their environment is mostly small; it may be a particular point in a town (a square, a building, a junction) or a neighbourhood. It is, therefore, particularly relevant to local planning. The problem is how to plan for good design and what to take into account when evaluating it.

### Factors that influence design

Design is not an independent entity. It is related to various elements, most of which are tangible and concrete, and which can be evaluated in a fairly objective way, whilst others are controversial, subjective and cultural. In order to understand the context in which designs are created, it will be useful to consider these elements here. None of the following elements works independently; they all combine to form a background for the designer.

*Technology*: The controversy over tall blocks would not exist if the lift had not been invented about a century ago. Though lifts were not the only cause of high rise buildings, they were a 'sine qua non'. The state of the building industry, the kinds of materials available, the capacity for mass

101

producing certain elements, affect the designer very significantly. Similarly, he is influenced by the current state of technology in associated fields, transport in particular. The automobile has undoubtedly had the biggest single impact on the environment in this century and, as a consequence, urban design has had to adapt to a new scale and a new approach to cities. In the future, growing shortages of oil may lead to new kinds of vehicles which could demand different kinds of roads to the ones we know today, and, therefore, once again new types of environments.

In general terms it can be said that methods of building construction are archaic: the brick and the standard window frame are about as far as mass production has gone. Attempts to apply new industrial technologies to the cities are few and, generally, unimaginative; they have led to dull, repetitive, unadaptable buildings—the high rise of prefabricated panels is the standard example. While in other fields, modern technology allows for a fair amount of flexibility in its application, it has not succeeded in doing so in the building context. The need for mass production has led to the abandonment of vernacular construction methods, but has not, as yet, led to a satisfactory replacement.

*Legislation:* The large number of existing regulations, by-laws, building standards, etc, which include planning legislation, limit considerably the scope of the designer. The list of official requirements that an architect has to satisfy is awesome, starting from land-use zoning, through density or plot-ratio, road engineers' requirements, fire precautions, daylight, ventilation and public health to the client's own demands. Special legislation affects buildings according to their use; for instance, public housing is controlled by the 'Housing cost yardstick' and 'Parker Morris standards', while industrial building is controlled by the Factories Act 1961. (9)

The load of legislation is so vast that it is even surprising that designers can find anything but a standard solution to any particular problem. It is to be hoped that local authorities will be more flexible than in the past in the way they apply the regulations. It is significant that in most cases, when an interesting building is erected, at least some of the regulations are found to have been waived.

*Economics*: To assume that good design can be as cheap as bad design is a fallacy. Quality depends on good materials, careful detailing and finishings, fine landscaping etc, all of which cost money. Only in the 'picturesque vernacular' can cheap construction be as pleasant, or more so, as expensive; in an industrial society, pressures are too many and good environments cost money. Private developers want to maximise their profits and, therefore, try to get the highest possible plot-ratio, to use standardised units and materials which are easy to maintain, and avoid trimmings. Only rarely will enlightened developers provide amenities or

102

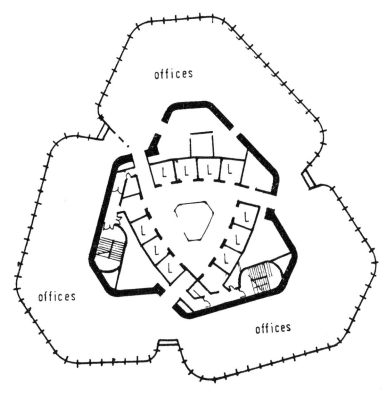

Fig 15: Design used to enhance a corporate image whilst also contributing to the townscape. Typical floor plan in the National Westminster Bank in the City of London.

erect exceptionally good buildings, more often for prestige reasons. In the United States, this kind of approach is widespread and has successfully endowed a number of cities with interesting environments, but in Britain, in recent times, this approach has been largely limited to financial institutions in the City of London or the occasional public corporation. (10)

Public developers, on the other hand, possess restricted funds and their expenditure is controlled by bureaucratic diktat. A housing architect constrained between minimum (Parker Morris) and maximum (Yardstick) standards, has an extremely narrow margin which does not allow, save in very exceptional cases, the addition of trimmings that could make a world of difference to a development scheme. The consequence can be seen not only in public housing, but also in such dreary places as pedestrian underpasses. It is probably fair to say that economic constraints are the most important influence on the standard of design.

103

*Location*: Any architect knows that site appraisal is the first activity that he should undertake when commissioned to design a scheme. It is not the same to design for an urban environment as for a rural one, on a mountain site or on the bank of a river. A long list of elements has to be taken into account and will vary from the nature of the local materials to the kind of surrounding buildings, from the ownership of the land to the orientation of the site. These items are generally those covered by 'site planning' exercises. (11)

*Tradition*: This mainly affects the way people react to a particular development and, therefore, the type of design that can be produced. For instance, the typical British family expectation in relation to housing is of a detached house—the result of many generations of conditioning. With increased living standards, this translates into a bungalow with garden and space for the car and, therefore, a low density environment of which suburbia is the main representation. High rise blocks are frowned upon, considered undesirable and so no effort is put into trying to improve them.

Another consequence of traditional thinking is the spread of 'conservation'. Old and known environments come to be regarded by definition as better than new ones. There is no confidence in the capacity of contemporary designers to produce satisfactory environments and, therefore, existing buildings are preserved, sometimes beyond rationality. The great advantage of old buildings is often their flexibility of adaptation to new uses, but this is not unlimited and forcing it for the sake of 'conservation' may produce sterile or inefficient results. This attitude, however, is not surprising since it is mainly a modern reaction to decades of aggressive destruction of many valuable parts of the architectural heritage.

In general, tradition is in conflict with innovation and can lead to excessive prudence. Architects knowing what the planning officer or the committee will allow will not even attempt a solution different from those already tested elsewhere.

*Taste*: This is the most imponderable factor of all and it is closely related to tradition. There is little consensus on what constitutes good or bad design, even when in general terms there is a common tradition in a society. Various groups will react differently, as is suggested in the quotations at the beginning of this chapter. Taste changes with time and what was considered good design at a certain period is censured in the next. The puritan attitudes of the modern architectural movement, with its misleading motto of 'form follows function', produced bare, undecorated buildings where no function at all was expressed, and which eventually developed into the 'brutalist' concept and their vilification of baroque Victorian architecture. As a reaction against it, contemporary designers and critics now advocate more elaborate buildings, praise the over-decoration of the Victorians, and even the aggressively commercial and

104

Fig 16: Controversial buildings of today may be the listed buildings of tomorrow: The National Theatre on the South Bank. Photograph by John Pulham.

transitory architecture of the American highway. (12) A persistent economic depression could well swing the balance back towards a more austere style.

As the last comment indicates, taste is affected by other factors in society. Public taste can also be influenced; if people can be conditioned to buy one kind of soap powder and to prefer one kind of car to another, there is no reason why advertising cannot condition the public to accept or choose a certain kind of urban environment. And indeed, the popular press, as well as design 'experts', often condemn certain buildings or environments through their negative comments about them—London's South Bank complex and Brunswick Square in Bloomsbury are two examples which will probably remain as architectural landmarks of the second half of this century, although both were fiercely attacked when first completed.

## Requirements
How can guidance to designers be incorporated in the local plan, and what criteria would the development control officer take into account when evaluating a scheme? These questions are basic in trying to achieve a more positive role for planning; but before answering them, we must define

what we expect from the built environment. In broad terms, there are two major all-embracing requirements.

Firstly the scheme has to function. The Sale of Goods Act 1893 as amended by the Supply of Goods (Implied Terms) Act 1973 requires that when a product is sold, it must be fit for the purpose for which goods of that kind are normally used: thus a bucket must not leak. (13) Similarly, a building has to function according to the activity that is to take place in it; but also, it has to be ensured that it is not hindering the good functioning of the surrounding area. Vehicular access, parking, massing and height—these are some of the matters that have to be considered, and they will have to be included in a documentary study. Additionally, the functioning of the building is related to items already listed—it has to be economic, to make good use of the existing technology, to take account of its location, presumably the client who has commissioned the building will demand that these requirements are satisfied. The following statement by G Burke is a good example of practical, common sense and unsentimental evaluation of a scheme—Runcorn's Shopping City: 'It is not a work of art and was not intended to be; it looks like what it is, a logical container for a complex of everyday activity, and it promises to work efficiently and well.' (14)

The second requirement is that the scheme has to give aesthetic satisfaction, not only to those using it, but also to those seeing it. For some, this is no different from the previous requirement, since it can be argued that no building truly functions without giving aesthetic satisfaction, but that is a controversial argument and, for the sake of clarity, it is considered separately.

The built environment is full of symbols, some accidental, some intentional, and these have to be recognised and evaluated. Unfortunately, the psychology of form is not a well developed discipline, and town-planners lack even simple criteria by which to pursue the matter of form. An example may clarify this point—the outstanding feature of a European town during the Middle Ages was its cathedral; during the age of absolutism, the monarch's palace replaced it. In the nineteenth century, the prominent elements of the cities reflected the achievements of the industrial bourgeoisie, eg the railway stations. Today, the tallest buildings are the offices of international corporations and banks. In each case, the dominant powers in society were reflected in the urban scene. On the other hand, consider a well known building such as the United Nations headquarters in New York. What is its outstanding feature? What does the public remember of it? It is the curtain-wall slab-building, the bureaucratic centre, and not the much lower and modest auditorium which is the true forum of the United Nations.

This does not imply, however, that every new building has to make a formal statement. On the contrary, according to G Burke: 'The urban architecture normally appreciated by the townsman is that which does not compel him to look at it: the kind that forms a quiet, even slightly self-effacing, background to everyday life. . .' (15)

This anonomity in itself is a statement about our society. Charles Jencks has suggested that one of the major failures of modern architecture has been to adopt a universal language (the 'International style') which applies to all places and all functions, thus losing any sense of identity and confusing the symbols, so that a block of flats looks like a block of offices, an art gallery like a bunker, a school like a factory. The user and the viewer are thus misled and have trouble in identifying with the environment. (16) Kevin Lynch indicates how people relate to certain aspects of the urban landscape and how they need an environment which facilitates image-making—districts with a particular character, paths which lead somewhere, and nodes which are 'distinct and unforgettable places'. (17) Similarly, work on people's perception of places, such as that of Brian Goodey, indicates how people react to their environment. (18)

A pilot survey in Reading undertaken by students of Reading University tried to investigate what people saw as the 'character' of the city's central area, and how they reacted to its redevelopment. It was a study with direct application to people's lives, but the results showed a great deal of indifference and a basic opposition to change. (19) Semiotics, the study of symbols, is attracting more interest among planners, and research in the field is increasing. (20) Unfortunately, although it explains and catalogues the reactions of people to their environment, most of the work does not give guidelines on how it should be evaluated, or how good environment can be produced. S Harrison, reviewing *A pilot study in Sunderland* rightly asked: 'What is the purpose of identifying people's perception of the extent of the town centre?' (21) But C Steinitz, suggested that 'Designers must not underestimate the efficacy of educating people to know and use the characteristics of their environment.' (22)

## Guidelines

The practical conclusion appears to be negative if not pessimistic. If consensus on what constitutes good design cannot be arrived at, beyond certain basic 'objective' elements, then refusing a planning application on aesthetic grounds is irrational and unfair. The results of twenty years of aesthetic controls have, arguably, avoided some disasters; but they certainly have not encouraged good design. Comparing the results to those in a country where no such controls exist—the USA for example—it must be concluded that they are at best less than effective, and at worst they stifle designers' initiative. Most unfortunately, the control at the moment is ultimately in the hands of lay committees, which only leads—as the evidence shows—to mediocrity. The designer will know—and if not, the development control officer will tell him—what the committee will accept;

and this is the lowest common denominator of aesthetics—the bureaucratic solution that will offend nobody, but will not please anyone either. As N Beddington said: 'May it be that architects may sometimes be appointed not for creative ability but to produce work which is sufficiently non-controversial to slip through the planning net without too much difficulty?' (23)

The complete abandonment of aesthetic controls is probably unacceptable, and the Dobry report (24) indicated this. Instead, some authorities have appointed 'architects' advisory panels'; others have 'conservation area advisory committees' for their conservation areas. These advise on the aesthetic merits of schemes presented to them. Whilst this approach may be preferable from the point of view of the resulting design, it can be dangerous to have architects judging the work of their colleagues. Additionally, it does not give guidelines to designers about what is required from them and, therefore, does not offer a positive approach. Gerald Burke is in favour of this (very elitist) approach: 'That architects' designs should be considered only by their professional "equals" ought not to be in dispute.' (25) and he goes further in suggesting that only people with a qualification in architectural design should be allowed to submit designs, which should then only be judged by equally qualified officials.

Conservation areas are probably the easiest to legislate for. If the character which it is intended to preserve and enhance has been clearly identified, guidelines can be given to designers in no uncertain terms. An example is the following quote from the Richmond town centre plan: 'Strong elements such as gable roofs or bay windows may be very important to the townscape of an area and may offer the basis for a well integrated design solution: a dull, poorly designed rectangular box would not be considered a positive contribution in an area of ornate Victorian villas.' (26)

Another fairly precise guideline is to be found in the Wallingford local plan: 'In general, synthetic materials will not be acceptable in the conservation area, and rainwater goods, roofs, shop fronts and fascias should be constructed in the appropriate natural material.' (27)

From the methodological point of view, the Windsor town centre plan suggests that 'all planning applications of a substantial nature should be accompanied by a "photomontage" type presentation in addition to the usual plans required'. (28) Additionally, a number of local authorities proposes to use 'Article 4 directions' in their conservation areas. These have the effect of removing the right to carry out certain otherwise permitted developments, including decorating; and, therefore, authorities can indicate with precision what kind of development they would allow. (29) Design guidelines are mentioned as an important follow-up to the plan in almost all conservation areas. In the case of the plan for Camden, the first of London's borough plans to be published, policy guidelines for each

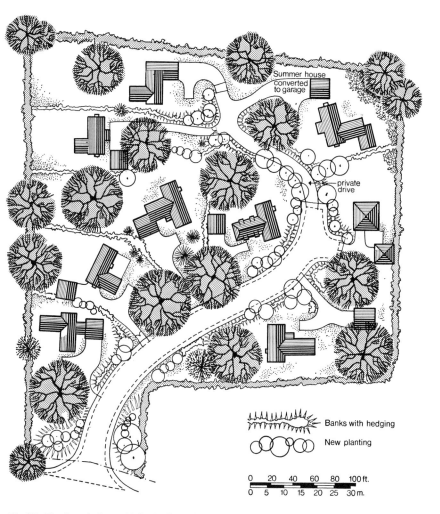

Within the figure:
Summer house converted to garage

private drive

Banks with hedging

New planting

0　20　40　60　80　100 ft.
0　5　10　15　20　25　30 m.

Fig 17: The first design guidelines: Essex County Council Design Guide for Residential Areas, 1973.

conservation area are part of the main document and include sketches of what would be 'desirable' and 'undesirable' design features, and of features to be respected.

Outside conservation areas, various kinds of guidelines exist. Probably the best known, because it was the first of its kind, is the Essex county council's *Design guide for residential areas*, which was followed by a series of similar documents in Cheshire, East Hants, Preseli district, etc. Starting with housing, the Essex guide lays certain 'performance criteria' that a development has to satisfy in order to be approved; these relate to the lay-out of a housing estate, to aspects of privacy, accessibility, and to purely visual criteria such as the use of materials, proportionality, units of elevation, rural versus urban-spatial organisation, etc. The final section of the guide attempts to fuse all the elements into case studies, thus giving examples for the developers to follow. It is made clear that the council does not want to see these imitated all over the county, but the danger exists nevertheless—developers, knowing what will be acceptable may decide to play safe and copy the models. In the last two years, some estate agents' publicity for developments makes a point of describing schemes as 'designed to Essex guide'; and this is felt to be a proof of success for this kind of approach, since it expresses approval by the general public. (30)

A criticism of the second generation guidelines that followed Essex has been that, instead of concentrating on general aspects of the townscape, they give details of the buildings themselves. This then adds to the fears of architects that design guides stifle innovation, that they are too traditional in outlook, and that in the end they will be just another kind of regulation to be complied with.

There exist variations on this approach, which, rather than give models that can be imitated, outline a general framework or limit themselves to performance criteria which will be considered by development control officers. G Burke points out the importance of expressions, such as 'will be discouraged' or 'should be treated', which are used in these guidelines and lists some of the criteria—mass and height, accord of material, contrast of form, matching of spirit, etc. (31) In sites of particular significance, or where coordination with adjoining buildings is particularly important, these frameworks can be more specific—shopping streets, for instance, can be very sensitive and canopy heights and widths, window shapes, materials, etc, may be specified.

Camden's plan includes a section called 'The environmental code' which 'is the first attempt to formalise the principles which will be applied in considering the physical aspects of developments.' The criteria are given separately for residential and non-residential development and deal with the accommodation, the layout and the neighbourhood impact. They are not limited to design, but, on this, it is stated (for instance): 'A high
110

1

Fig 18: Design guidelines Mark II: Cheshire. Cheshire County Council Design Aids, Housing: Roads, 1976.

111

standard of contemporary design will be expected except in cases of the replacement in replica of buildings which form part of a uniform terrace or row of villas.'

For the moment the code is mainly a formalisation of measures that have been used in the past, but it is suggested that it will be updated and augmented as and when necessary. The introduction also states that it will be applied flexibly: 'It is not to be interpreted as a collection of minimum standards each of which must be attained, but as a set of principles and objectives against which total performance should be optimised.' (32)

The Barnsley town centre Action Area plan has also adopted an interesting approach to this problem of control of the environment. They have produced a number of policies relating mainly to materials and mass and height of buildings, and applying differently to specific areas indicated on a series of supplementary maps:

'Building materials and forms in new developments will accord with the general principles laid down in the Proposals Map, Supplementary Map 1, Townscape Policy, Materials and Form.

This Map defines areas of pitched and flat roofed development, and indicates areas where certain materials predominate.' (33)

Another approach on a systematic site-to-site basis was suggested by John Minnett during a conference in 1974. Stage two of this approach, which formulates criteria to ensure a 'good fit' between the new land-use and particular systems, is relevant here. The development control officer is supposed to determine the 'level of intrusion' as it will affect primary interests (direct neighbours) and secondary interests (passers-by, regional bodies, the whole locality, others). From this analysis, criteria for granting permission for development on a particular site will be derived, and a development brief can be prepared. (34) The main disadvantage of this scheme is that it requires an outline planning application to initiate the study and, therefore, does not give guidance in advance. Additionally, it will be time-consuming. However, from this sort of approach, it may be possible to rationalise and anticipate elements which developers will have to take into account.

All the guidelines mentioned above apply mainly to private development. The built environment, however, is affected by a number of public elements which can influence the public's perception of it. Gordon Cullen, in his now classic *Townscape*, catalogued a number of these; and anyone walking with open eyes in any town or city, will be aware of them: street lighting, bus shelters and stops, telephone boxes, kiosks, railings, advertisements, a multitude of traffic signs, floor surfaces, etc. (35) They will also be aware of the scope for improvements. It is reasonable to suggest that local authorities have an obligation to apply aesthetic criteria to public street furniture, if they are to retain credibility when imposing

112

# Building design

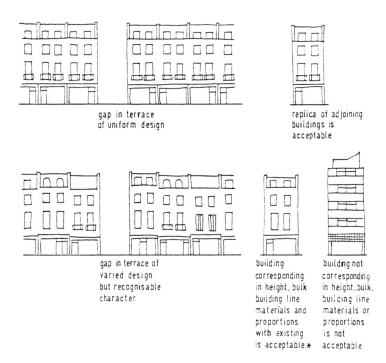

gap in terrace
of uniform design

replica of adjoining
buildings is
acceptable

gap in terrace of
varied design
but recognisable
character

building
corresponding
in height, bulk
building line
materials and
proportions
with existing
is acceptable*

building not
corresponding
in height, bulk,
building line
materials or
proportions
is not
acceptable

* this does not preclude a high standard of modern design

Fig 19: Different kind of guidelines applied to an urban area: Camden. Camden Borough Council: Environmental Code.

them on the private developer. Barnsley district council seems to have taken this into account. Its environment policies for the town centre include some proposals which will be their own or other public bodies' responsibility: 'The Barnsley Council will liaise with South Yorkshire County Council as highway authority to improve the standard of design, size and siting of signs, street furniture and surface materials.' (36)

Finally, a word of caution on guidelines. For the time being, they are not statutory documents and, therefore, cannot be considered as 'prima facie' evidence in an appeal, but only as 'other material considerations'. It is possible that, in the future, some of them will become part of a statutory local plan or a subject plan on their own right; but until then, or until the Secretary of State has shown willingness to accept and endorse their recommendations, they have to be used with caution.

# REFERENCES

1 Ministry of Housing and Local Government, *Development plans, a manual of form and content*, HMSO, London, 1970, chapter 1, para 1.8, p4.

2 MOHLG, Development Control Policy Note No 10. Design, HMSO, London, 1969, para 1.

3 M Broady, *Planning for people*, The Bedford Square Press of the National Council of Social Service, London, 1968, p14.

4 H Gans, *People and plans*, Basic Books, New York, 1968, Introduction, p2.

5 J Jacobs, *The death and life of great American cities*, Penguin Books, London, 1972.

6 O Newman, *Defensible space*, Macmillan, New York, 1972.

7 C Mercer, *Living in cities*, Penguin Books, London, 1975.

8 G Burke, *Townscapes*, Penguin Books, London, 1976, chapter 4, p 100.

9 The Housing Cost Yardstick was first introduced in the Housing Subsidies Act 1967 and is periodically reviewed by DOE Circulars. MOHLG, Homes for Today and Tomorrow, Report of a Subcommittee chaired by Sir Parker-Morris, LLB, HMSO, London, 1961.

10 The latest of its kind is the National Westminster Bank which in plan has the shape of the company's logo.

11 For additional literature on site planning, see K Lynch, *Site planning*, MIT Press, Cambridge, Mass, 1962; and Rubenstein, *A guide to site and environmental planning*, John Wiley and Sons, 1969.

12 See for instance R Banham, *Age of the masters: a personal view of Modern architecture*, Architectural Press, London, 1975; and *The new brutalism, ethic or aesthetic*, Architectural Press, London, 1966; also R Venturi, *Complexity and contradiction in architecture*, Architectural Press, London, 1977; and R Venturi, D S Brown and S Izenour, *Learning from Las Vegas: the forgotten symbolism of architectural form*, MIT Press, Cambridge, Mass, 1971.

13 The Supply of Goods (Implied Terms) Act 1973, c13, S14.

14 G Burke, op cit, chapter 6, p158.

15 G Burke, op cit, chapter 4, p98.

16 C Jencks, *The language of post-modern architecture*, Academy Editions, London, 1977, part one.

17 K Lynch, *The image of the city*, MIT Press, Cambridge, Mass, 1960. Also K Lynch, *What time is this place?*, MIT Press, Cambridge, Mass, 1972.

18 B Goodey, *Perception of the environment*, Occasional Paper No 17, Centre for Urban and Regional Studies, University of Birmingham, 1971. And also *Images of place: essays on environmental perceptions, communication and education*, Occasional Paper No 30, CURS, University of Birmingham, 1974.

19  G Burke, op cit, chapter 7 and appendix I.

20  Conference on Aesthetics Applied to the Creation of the Urban Landscape, Arc-et-Sénans, France, Sept 1973.

21  S Harrison, 'Perception related surveys for local authorities', review of a pilot study in Sunderland by Donely, Goodey and Menzies, in *The planner* vol 61, no 8, Sept/Oct 1975, p317.

22  C Steinitz, 'The meaning and the congruence of urban form and activity' in the *Journal of the American Institute of Planning*, July 1968, p246.

23  N Beddington, 'Mollycoddled into mediocrity', in *Built environment*, Dec 1973, p689.

24  G Dobry, Review of the Development Control System, Final Report to the DOE, HMSO, London, 1975.

25  G. Burke, op cit, chapter 8, p186.

26  London Borough of Richmond upon Thames, Richmond Town Centre, Action Area Plan Report, 1976, part 5, para 5.1.1, p72.

27  South Oxfordshire District Council, District plan for Wallingford, Draft Local Plan, 1976, chapter 7, para 7.3.2, p66.

28  Royal Borough of Windsor and Maidenhead, Windsor Town Centre, District Plan, Aug 1977, chapter 8, para 8.4.19, p40.

29  Article 4 Directions remove permitted development rights under the Town & Country Planning General Development Order 1973.  They are used mainly in conservation areas.

30  Essex County Council, *A design guide for residential areas*, 1973.  For a review and references of various guides, see DOE, Design Guidance Survey, London, 1976, survey undertaken by Llewellyn-Davis, Weeks Forestier, Walker and Bor.

31  G Burke, op cit, chapter 8, p186.

32  London Borough of Camden, A plan for Camden, The environmental code, Sept 1976, Introduction, and para 17 (i) on Residential Developments.

33  Barnsley Metropolitan Borough Council, Barnsley Town Centre Draft Action Area Plan, Feb 1978, Townscape and Environment, para E4, p83.

34  J Minett, 'A positive approach to development control', in *Proceedings of seminar M, development control and plan implementation*, PTRC Summer Annual Meeting, University of Warwick, July 1974, pp9-31.

35  G Cullen, *Townscape* The Architectural Press, London, 1961.

36  Barnsley MBC, op cit *Townscape and environment*, para E9, p84.

Chapter 9

# COMMUNITY AND NEIGHBOURHOOD

The definition of the word 'community' and its application to town-planning practice are the subjects of endless discussions amongst professionals and social scientists. Since this book is not a sociological treatise, it will not enter the polemic. It may, however, be useful for the practising town-planner to know how the concept has been used and/or abused, what relevance it may have had in developing the way professionals look at an area, and how useful it can be if properly researched and analysed.

The expression 'local plan' in itself, has, by definition, implications in spatial and social terms; it can refer to a neighbourhood, it can suggest a kind of community, or possibly both. When discussing the ways of fixing boundaries to an area, these concepts were at least briefly considered. The work of Lynch on the image of the city, and that of Goodey, Gould and Whyte on mental maps in particular, deal with the physical perception of communities and their relevance to planning. (1) This chapter reviews some of the main-stream approaches to 'community', its relationship to a locality or neighbourhood, and the application to town-planning, then the 'neighbourhood unit' idea, and its use in the planning of new towns; and, finally, the 'community action' movement which has developed in the last ten to fifteen years.

## Community
In 1955, G A Hillary uncovered ninety-four definitions of the word 'community', and he declared: 'All the definitions deal with people. Beyond this common basis, there is no agreement'. (2) Fortunately, most authorities find additional factors which are repeated in the majority of definitions: a geographical area shared by the members of the community; some sort of tie or interest that binds them together; a certain level of social interaction. These are not always all accepted, and the 'academic community' or the 'students' community' are examples of non-geographically based groups which use the noun. Even less locational is the term 'scientific community'; a scientist may communicate better with a colleague thousands of miles away but undertaking research on a similar subject than with his next door neighbour. (3) He may, however, at the same time, be part of locally-based associations on which his various allegiances have a bearing.

116

Some groups, whose members have common characteristics, only become communities in certain circumstances—for instance, when threatened by forces external to the group, whether area-based or not. In cities of the Third World for example, foreign groups are often known as 'colonies' or 'collectivities'; the 'British colony', the Jewish collectivity', are expressions often mentioned in the daily papers of cities such as Buenos Aires. Then, under stress, they suddenly become the British community or the Jewish community; with the implication that fairly loose ties become stronger in front of a common threat.

Although it could be inferred that non-territorial communities are of only marginal relevance to town-planning, this is not so for a number of reasons. To start with, they have a number of similarities with locally-based communities, and they may change and become area-based; the walled ghetto may—at least apparently—be a thing of the past, but the academic compound is still very present. It is a fact, even in major metropolitan areas, that ethnic or national minority concentrations are a significant element in the perception of community life. Additionally, new kinds of communities have appeared in the last fifteen years, often on the fringe of society—hippies, feminist separatists, communaders, etc. They, too, try to live in close proximity to each other as a form of self-protection, and their living patterns may be as different from the traditional community as those of the ethnic minorities.

Studies have tried to define what communities are and what constitutes a community. They try to answer questions such as, 'How do we recognise a community when we see one?' or 'What are the changes that have occured since the traditional community (eg the village) has been replaced by the city?' In P Mann's *An approach to urban sociology*, quotes from two differing authors, McIver and Lundberg, are summarised in general terms as including three main points: the community is geographically based; its members have a common life and interact; and a community is always relative to some other group, it is a matter of degree. (4)

Because of this last factor, an ideal type-concept of community has to be established and the level of approximation of real to ideal types can then be measured. Two completely different situations, such as an isolated village and an urban neighbourhood, can both be called communities, but they approximate to the ideal in different degrees.

At a more abstract level is the analysis of the concepts of 'Gemeinschaft' and 'Gesellschaft' in the work of F Tönnies. The imprecise translations of these words are given as 'community' and 'society'; and the duality is explained as including organic and natural life (family, sentiments, folkways) in one case, and mechanic and rational will (convention, legislation, public opinion) in the other. (5) Additional polarities in social organisations, as postulated by various authors, are also analysed by Mann, who concludes by putting forward the theory that these are not dichotomies, but part of a continuum. As people move from the village to the

117

city, Gemeinschaft dimishes and Gesellschaft becomes the dominant. (6)

Taking a historical perspective, this continuum can be made apparent. The village type of community is the primitive form of settlement, predominant in all pre-industrial societies. They are on the whole, self-sufficient and area-based and, as in Tönnies, Gemeinschaft; their ties include religion, work, family and culture. Kinship relationships are strong, roles clearly defined, leadership accepted and change slight; an additional and fundamental factor, isolation, gives the village its sense of community. The urban-industrial revolution, however, resulted in increased specialisation and the decline of autonomous local communities, while national or international forms of association developed. It is not necessary to move to the urban environment to observe the change: villagers are exposed to the same mass media as the urbanites, their lives are linked to that of other villages, towns or cities; the price of their produce is regulated by another kind of community, the EEC, in which they have very little say; the kinship ties have become looser and, in many cases, the village has been invaded by commuters or searchers for second homes.

In the city, the same phenomenon has occured, albeit in different ways. Communities in this environment have often been associated with working-class areas or among deprived minority groups. Young and Willmott's study of East London is probably the classic text on this subject in Britain. (7) Here, as in the village, kinship ties were strong and there was a high degree of homogeneity of income, class, education, habits and aspirations, all of which led to a 'community spirit'. This changed as people were dispersed to suburbs with different physical patterns—less conducive to social interaction—and with new demands on the people. Various authors noted that the 'community spirit' did not necessarily disappear, but the relationships changed. In certain cases, they had to become more formalised; for instance, through constituted associations, because a new code of behaviour was not readily available. (8)

As can be realised, the changes in communications were one of the elements that sustained the dispersal of communities, and it is worth noting in passing that the two words have the same root. When people can travel from one end of the country to the other in less than a day, and see the same television programme in any part of the country at the same instant, boundaries of close knit communities tend to dissolve. A family's place of residence is just that; not every member of the family develops all his activities in or near that place. Most likely, the various members work in different parts of town, have friends somewhere else, and do a proportion of their shopping far from the home. With rising incomes, the radii of operations increase and, for certain groups, friends may be hundreds of miles away but in easy reach by dial-direct telephone.

Unfortunately, it is not possible to show statistically how mobility

118

has changed and affected the life of communities, for it is only since the 1961 census that information about length of residence at a particular address has been gathered. The migration waves from country to cities during the second part of the nineteenth century have probably not been equalled during this present century; but figures are not available. R M Pritchard in *Housing and the spatial structure of the city* has indicated that the residential mobility in 1870 Leicester was higher than it is today, at least amongst the working-classes, but moves were generally restricted to a short distance. (9) Young and Willmott showed that until the post-war rehousing resulting from local authority redevelopment, East End families lived for generations in the same area, close to their relatives and friends. (10)

In spite of the changes outlined in the previous paragraphs, the local community has not lost its significance altogether. Criticising M Webber's idea that there is no longer a community of place, Colin Bell and H Newby stated: 'An interest community is an essentially single-stranded relationship, whereas community is about multi-stranded relationship. Most people do *not* move most of the time. . . Where *do* they send their children to school?' (11)

Even in large cities we hear of 'urban villagers', and people do talk about the area they live in with a certain feeling of belonging to somewhere in particular. In urban situations, these territorial communities tend to be larger than the traditional ones, and less easily defined; they can reach populations of 50,000 people or more, as in the case of Willmott's Dagenham. Their identity can be socially or physically based, or both; the more different from other areas and the more isolated the area and its people are, the easier it will be to identify. A family moving into a city will—if it can—choose the area where its members are more likely to find their peers from an ethnic, social, religious or intellectual point of view.

Turning more specifically to the community of place, other authorities accept that there is such a thing and study its characteristics. An example is found in the work of Park and Burgess, which analyses the locational segregation of various residential communities within a city. (12) These and other ecological theories take for granted the existence of communities with certain common features, based on income or class, which look for their 'natural area' as their habitat; these can be sectors, concentric circles, or a mixture of both. Other studies analyse specific characteristics of communities—the effects of moving from an inner area to a suburb (Young and Willmott)(13) on the patterns of relationships in a community; or the effects of television on leisure patterns of a community; or the behaviour of particular communities (Frankenberg). (14) When considering the specific habitat of a community, the term 'neighbourhood' may be more appropriate and it will, therefore, be considered now.

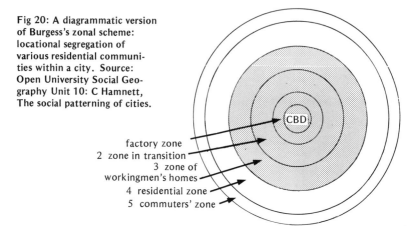

Fig 20: A diagrammatic version of Burgess's zonal scheme: locational segregation of various residential communities within a city. Source: Open University Social Geography Unit 10: C Hamnett, The social patterning of cities.

factory zone
2 zone in transition
3 zone of workingmen's homes
4 residential zone
5 commuters' zone

CBD

## Neighbourhoods

'Greenwich Village, like Chelsea and the Left Bank, is the sort of background which tends to be even phonier on the screen than it is in reality'. (15)

Thus started a review of a film in the *Sunday times*, and that comment echoes many similar criticisms of the artificiality of certain 'urban villages'. In spite of these comments, they exist in the minds of people and are recongised, even though their boundaries may be fuzzy, or their characteristics may be seen differently by various observers.

Each large metropolis probably has its Bohemian area, where the local Jane Jacobs lives and observes from the window, and of which much is written; but there are other neighbourhoods, less publicised but similarly meaningful to their users. (16) People know to which neighbourhood they belong, even though they may have difficulty in describing it. 'I live in Bow', or 'I come from Fulham', are credible answers to the question 'Where do you come from?', put to Londoners.

People may, in fact, answer differently depending on whom they are talking to: a local, a tourist, an official, or a casual acquaintance. A number of studies have tried to elucidate whether it is the physical or human characteristics which define the neighbourhood in the minds of people. It will be accepted here that it is a combination of both: the community resides in a neighbourhood. The English language does not have a word like 'quartier' or 'barrio', which in French and Spanish describe the physical area of the neighbourhood, without the social connotation of the English word. Whatever the sociological definition given, it is the family wanting to move into an area or out of it, or having lived in it for a number of years, who will be perceiving it and experiencing it; and it is in relation to this potential family that we should be considering the neighbourhood.

P Mann stated that 'In Britain, the idea of the "neighbourhood" is
120

almost synonymous with the study of working-class housing estates.'
(17) This bias may have distorted the view of what a neighbourhood is,
so for our purposes, a few of the characteristics will be mentioned. It will
be seen as a distinct geographical area, with fairly clear boundaries, a
certain degree of homogeneity in the buildings—given by their size, style,
state of repair, tenure, etc—and most probably also a certain degree of
social homogeneity—given by the households' size, age, class and race.
These variables were considered in chapter two when looking at the ways
of defining an area. Ruth Glass suggests another way of defining a neighbourhood—by analysing the catchment areas for different institutions, such
as schools and shops. When these coincide, and correspond to a distinct
locality with a certain population, this locality is a neighbourhood. (18)

For the individual or the family, the neighbourhood provides social
links, in varying degrees of closeness, and a series of services near the
home. As Mann has very well described, these links and services may
either be very important or almost irrelevant, according to the individual's
social class, income, sex and age. In most cases, however, the neighbourhood is a place of retreat from the 'total' urban life, a kind of known
and secure refuge from the wide wild world. This feeling increases with
length of residence and, in parallel, it is possible that the boundaries of the
perceived neighbourhood widen as a larger territory is explored and incorporated to the familiar one. If the individual does not like his/her
neighbourhood, it can assume negative characteristics and be threatening
and unpleasant; the person will want to leave the area, but will still recognise it as an entity. Otherwise, it will be seen in relation to the city, what
an individual's own room may be to the rest of the house, the familiar,
the safe, the comfortable. (19) This is particularly true in very urban
environments, whether working-, middle- or upper-class. The local shopkeeper very quickly recognises his local customers in Manhattan, in central
Paris and in Soho. A report on neighbourhood preservation in New York
city makes the following statement: 'In a city in flux, New York's neighbourhoods provide a much needed source of continuity. Although their
boundaries are imprecise and shifting, they are physical manifestations of
shared social values, shared culture and shared institutions.' (20) This
seems to be an appropriate description of the importance of the neighbourhood in today's urban environment.

In 1968, the GLC published a plan for Covent Garden, an area covering
about ninety-six acres of central London, embracing parts of two adjacent
boroughs and bounded by main roads. (21) It is very unlikely that anyone
except those immediately around the Covent Garden central market
buildings would have recognised that area as a neighbourhood, let alone a
community. However, as protest against the plan got under way, the
Covent Garden Community Association was formed and, for a while at
least, there was definitely a feeling of belonging to some special group

of those living in the designated area or in any way affected by the plan. Ten years later, this feeling has faded somewhat, but it still exists and has, in some ways, become institutionalised. Covent Garden is recognised as a neighbourhood by insiders and outsiders in a way in which it was not before; it has its own neighbourhood festival, its independent newsheet, a social centre and a number of active local organisations. It may be worth noting that, for an inner city area, the population density in Covent Garden is extremely low (when the whole area is taken into account) and the total population itself very small: there are less than 3,000 residents in the ninety-six acres of the plan area. Because of the plan and the struggle against it, people have met and now greet each other in the streets, as in a traditional village. At the same time, the social controls that would exist in a village do not exist here, and the anonymity of the great city can be maintained if desired.

In the adjacent London borough of Camden, planners presented, together with the borough plan, a series of special area plans and tried to relate their general policies to some kind of neighbourhood perceived on the ground. This is a useful tool which may help create a community feeling in an area, and it is increasingly used by authorities preparing local plans. (22)

In 1923, an American community worker, Clarence Perry, first used the expression 'neighbourhood unit'. Since then, a large proportion of the discussions about neighbourhood and community in town-planning has centred on this concept. What Perry meant by it was 'that area which embraces all the public facilities and conditions required by the average family for its comfort and proper development within the vicinity of its dwellings'. (23) Six characteristics were necessary to define a neighbourhood unit—its size (related to a primary school); its boundaries, which should be distinct; the open spaces needed for recreation; its centre, comprising institutions such as a hall, library, school and church; its shopping districts located on the periphery; and its internal road network. By definition, this is a physical description; and, by its implications— that the residents could feel part of a community and like it, it is wholly deterministic. At the heart of the definition is the 'average family'—a difficult concept to accept when one- and two-person households, which statistically are just as numerous as the larger households, are probably not considered as families by planners and housing managers.

The neighbourhood unit was taken by the Garden City movement in this country and incorporated into the design criteria of the post-war new towns; residential areas were split into units separated from each other by open spaces, each one with its local centre and school. Through traffic would be excluded form the neighbourhoods, and they would be linked with each other and with the main town centre by radials and ring roads. It was assumed that social interaction would thus develop within each
122

neighbourhood, and that people would have a feeling of belonging to a special place. The identity of each neighbourhood would be emphasised by design features. (24)

An additional objective was incorporated in the British new towns—that of achieving 'balanced' communities, where different social classes would be mixed and leadership would emerge naturally. Apart from the difficulties of defining balance, this went directly against the natural trend of segregation which takes place in cities, and it seems that new towns have not achieved this egalitarian objective. In fact, one of the main criticisms of new towns is that they have not absorbed a typical cross-section of society, and that they perpetuate class segregation by excluding underprivileged groups. A look at traditional communities which, supposedly, have been successful, would not show such a balance; and it is not surprising that this objective has been dropped. The only advantage that has been proved to be real is that a balanced, or mixed, community— can support a wider range of services—but whether these will be equally used by the various social strata remains to be seen.

According to N Dennis, the neighbourhood community idea, as represented by the unit, is an ideological tool of control. It disperses the mass of working people and divides it into self-contained and inward-looking groups; it distracts potential leaders from looking at wider problems and leads them to concentrate on narrow community affairs. It also influences people into greater conformism, since there is an immediate control group with which they have to interact. (25)

Whatever the criticisms of the neighbourhood unit and the transformations which the concept has undergone, it has not been abandoned as a planning instrument. The latest of the new towns, Milton Keynes, allows for freedom of choice in relation to services and, in the words of Llewellyn Davies, this leads to the rejection of the neighbourhood unit. (26) Similarly, the report on the never-built Hook new town had considered the unit as inappropriate. However, in both cases, the plans show something very similar to it, called the 'super-block' in the case of Hook, albeit with a different distribution of services, centres and schools, and less clearly defined boundaries. (27)

A sense of belonging, a community spirit or thriving neighbourliness, probably cannot be achieved by disposing buildings in a certain way on the ground. For example, a community hall in every housing estate will not necessarily develop community spirit in the local residents. Jean K Perraton has indicated that there may be conflicts in the objectives that planners have tried to fulfil: close neighbourly contacts often go against wider community involvement; the friendliness of the slums does not work well with 'active participation in purposive associations of a middle-class suburb'. (28) Social planners have probably made a mistake in expecting too much from the application of such concepts as the neighbourhood

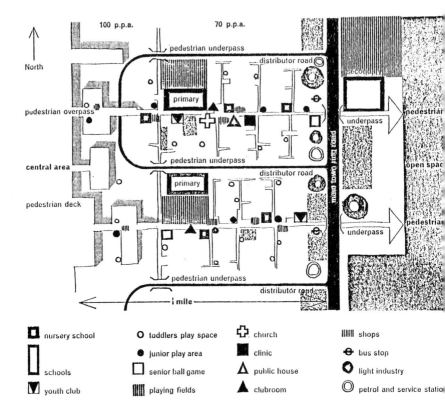

100 p.p.a.    70 p.p.a.

North

pedestrian underpass
distributor road

primary

pedestrian overpass

central area

pedestrian underpass

distributor road

primary

pedestrian deck

underpass

pedestrian

open space

pedestrian

underpass

pedestrian underpass
distributor road
½ mile

■ nursery school          O toddlers play space     ✚ church          ⅢⅢ shops

▯ schools                 ● junior play area        ■ clinic          ⊖ bus stop

                          ▢ senior ball game        ▲ public house    O light industry

▼ youth club              ⅢⅢ playing fields         ▲ clubroom        ◎ petrol and service station

Fig 21: In Hook New Town, the neighbourhood unit became the 'super block'.
Source: LCC, The Planning of a New Town, 1961. By courtesy of the Greater
London Council.

unit. As P Mann has said, 'The neighbourhood unit has been seen primarily as a tool for social reform or social work'. (29)

However, in purely practical terms, the unit has its use and can be
helpful if properly applied. This means planning so that needs can be
satisfied locally; in other words, that the primary schools, the shops, the
administrative centre or, in some cases, the employment centre, can be
reached with minimum effort. This requires a certain population to support the services and a certain level of compactness. Beyond this, the precise form, the relative location of land-uses, the boundaries, will vary from
case to case and be either rigidly or loosely defined. They may develop into
communities, or result in what is sometimes called 'partial' communities—
that is, fulfilling some, but not all, of the needs of the family.
124

## Community action

'The community is dead, long live the community', would be quite an appropriate way of describing what has been happening in the past fifteen years in urban areas. A review of existing literature on the subject indicates that, for most authors, the community as traditionally known does not exist any more. Mostly, they bemoan the fact that suburbia, council estates, dying rural centres, all lack community spirit, which can only be found occasionally in small pockets of surviving working-class neighbourhoods.

However, 'community action groups' have been started all over the country, to such an extent that, in 1972, a magazine *Community action* started publication and is still in existence today. It is worth quoting from the editorial of issue no 1: 'Our involvement and discussion with community action groups throughout the country has demonstrated the need for a magazine of this kind. . . By drawing together local issues and analysing them, it will be possible to suggest new national policies and ways of making them effective. . . It is hoped that the magazine will act as a catalyst in various cities to form groups of those involved in community action.' (30)

Any issue of the magazine at random will confirm that community action groups exist throughout the country and in very varied circumstances. They seem to get involved in all kind of problems—lack of play groups; fighting against a motorway proposal or for housing rights; producing a local magazine; caring for battered wives, etc; the list is seemingly endless. The kinds of areas where these groups arise also vary immensely, from poor and run-down residential areas in the inner city, to a 'nice' village in Wales. The main element they have in common is that in almost every case they appear in response to some sort of public authority action which is seen as a threat to a number of people or to the locality, and the action group starts from there, on the defensive. The public 'provocation' can be negative or passive as well—for example, the non-provision of a service or the non-prevention of some nuisance.

Another characteristic which is fairly common is that, at least at the beginning, the action group's leaders tend to be articulate and middle-class —often newcomers to the area, and often, too, professionals like planners or architects. In a report on community organisation, *Community action* advises on 'forming an action group': 'The problem is, of course, who organises the first meeting since someone has to take an initiative. There is no short answer to this problem, except to say that if you feel an action group is needed, get some local people together to form a nucleus who will take on responsibility for organising the meeting.' (31)

As was mentioned before in relation to Covent Garden, a 'real' community may develop where one was not identifiable before as a result of the creation of the action group, and this may survive well beyond the original issue. This happens partly because contacts are made during the 'action' period and new relationships develop; common interests and new issues are discovered, a meeting place may be found, people assume roles, etc. In this sense it could be argued that the antagonism originated by the public action has healthy repercussions, since it manages to recreate conditions which were lamented as lost and irretrievable.

We may thus summarise the kinds of communities the planners have to deal with and the roles they can have. In considering a local area, whether urban or rural, the local planner must not expect to see a perfect 'Gemeinschaft', nor should he try to create or recreate one. He should, however, ascertain what kinds of links exist in a neighbourhood and how it is perceived by its residents or users, and how by outsiders. Groups may or may not be permanent and the ties between their members may be very loose. The planner should allow for a variety of associations to flourish and/or evolve. In that sense, rigid housing standards which do not allow forms of sharing, other than amongst members of one family, are typical obstacles to the formation of any but the very standard kind of community. By drawing boundaries and preparing plans for areas, planning can emphasise the specific characteristics of a neighbourhood, reinforce it and allow it to thrive, instead of adopting a uniform pattern for all locations. The already mentioned example of Camden's special area plans is a good example of what can be done.


## REFERENCES

1  K Lynch, *The image of the city*, MIT Press, Cambridge, Mass, 1975. B. Goodey, *Perception of the environment*, Occasional paper No 17, Centre of Urban and Regional Studies, University of Birmingham, 1971. P R Gould and R R White, *Mental maps*, Penguin Books, 1974.

2  G A Hillery, 'Definitions of community, areas of agreement' in *Rural sociology*, 20, no 2, pp115-125, 1955.

3  M Webber, 'The urban place and the non-place realm', in *Explorations into urban structure*, (various authors), University of Philadelphia Press, 1967, pp108-132.

4  P Mann, *An approach to urban sociology*, Routledge and Kegan Paul Ltd, London 1970, chapter 7, p187.

5  F Tönnies, *Community and society*, Harper & Row, New York, 1963. See also J R Mellor, *Urban sociology in an urbanised society*, Routledge and Kegan Paul, London, 1978, pp178-181.

6  P Mann, op cit, pp207-209.

7  M Young and P Willmott, *Family and kinship in East London*, Penguin Books, London, 1974.

8  For a survey of the work of Louis Wirth, G Simmel, Tönnies, the Chicago School, etc, see J R Mellor, op cit. Also, R Durant, 'Community Association in a London housing estate', in R Pahl's *Readings in urban sociology*, Pergamon, 1968.  See also C Bell and H Newby, *Community studies*, George Allen & Unwin, 1971, chapters 2 and 7.

9  R M Pritchard, *Housing and the spatial structure of the city*, Cambridge University Press, 1976, chapter 3.

10  M Young and P Willmott, op cit, chapters 2 and 8.

11  C Bell and H Newby, op cit, p18.

12  E W Burgess, 'The growth of the city', in R E Park, E W Burgess and R D McKenzie (eds), *The city*, University of Chicago Press, 1925.  And R E Park and E W Burgess, *Introduction to the science of society* University of Chicago Press. 1921.

13  Young and Willmott, op cit.

14  R Frankenberg, *Communities in Britain: social life in town and country*, Penguin Books, London, 1967.

15  A Brien, 'The voice of the village' in *The Sunday times* weekly review, February 6 1977.

16  J Jacobs, *The death and life of great American cities*, Penguin Books, London 1972.  A number of anecdotes and observations are based on Hudson Street in Greenwich Village in Manhattan.

17  P Mann, op cit, chapter 6, p149.

18  R Glass, *The social background of a plan: a study of Middlesbrough*, Routledge and Kegan Paul, London, 1948.

19  P Mann, op cit, chapter 6, pp150-170.

20  Comprehensive Planning Workshop, Neighbourhood Preservation in New York City, City Planning Commission, New York, 1973, chapter 1, p7.

21  Consortium of Greater London Council, City of Westminster and London Borough of Camden, Covent Garden's Moving, Covent Garden Area Draft Plan, 1968.

22  London Borough of Camden, A plan for Camden—Draft Plan, Sept 1976.  A number of separate papers were prepared with 'special area policy' as a title, followed by the specific area, eg, Hatton Garden, Clerkenwell, Legal Precinct, University area, etc, or for action areas such as Camden Town.

23  C Perry, 'The neighbourhood unit formula', in *Urban housing*, The Free Press, New York, 1966, pp94-109.  Originally mentioned in 'A community unit in city planning and development', a paper delivered in 1923.

24  For British New Towns, see F J Osborn and A Whittick, *The new towns*, Leonard Hill, 1969, re-edited in 1977.

25  N Dennis, 'The popularity of the neighbourhood idea', In R Pahl's *Readings in urban sociology*, Pergamon, Oxford, 1968.

26  Lord Llewellyn-Davies, 'Changing goals in design: The Milton Keynes example', in *New towns: the British experience*, H Evans (ed), Charles Knight, 1972, pp102-116.

27  London County Council, *The planning of a new town*, London, 1961. Chapter 5 deals with residential areas, the unsuitability of the neighbourhood unit and their replacement by super-blocks.

28  J K Perraton, 'Community planning', in the *Journal of the Town Planning Institute*, vol 53, no 3, March 1967, pp95-98.

29  P Mann, op cit, p150.

30  *Community action* no 1, February 1972, editorial statement.

31  'Community Organisation: Forming an Action Group' in *Community action*, no 12, Feb/March 1974, p24.

Chapter 10

# PRACTICAL CONSIDERATIONS

It is appropriate to conclude this work with a consideration of some of the practical situations which will most frequently be encountered in a local plan. Three of the four following sections deal with specific land uses and one with movement.

Though it is unlikely that a local plan will be concerned with one kind of activity to the exclusion of all others, it is often the case that one does predominate and/or is the main motivator for the plan. The choice made here is principally based on the frequency with which plans deal with particular activities—housing and shopping top the list, and traffic management problems are often dealt with in conjunction with them. Though not as frequent, recreation is increasingly seen as an important topic for local planning, both in areas of deprivations and in those with tourist attraction.

## Housing

The planning profession had its roots in the housing problem, and the provision of housing has always been at the centre of planners' preoccupations. It is, therefore, not surprising that so much professional writing has been dedicated to the subject.

However, a review of this literature seems to point in two directions. One is theoretical, dealing with the policies of housing in general and fairly abstract terms. This leads, for instance, to arguments about the pros and cons of redevelopment as opposed to rehabilitation; or, at another level, to the establishment of a housing programme for a local authority in terms of numbers of dwellings started per annum. (1) The other direction that literature seems to pursue is that of the detailed site layouts, mainly the concern of architects and engineers; this leads, for instance, to recommendations on the best arrangements of houses around a communal access, or to space-standards such as those of the Parker Morris report. (2) In between, authors have, of course, dealt with a number of other housing issues; but it has not been easy to pitch research, theory or policy to a particular area scale—local in this case. There has been a reluctance to do so, probably based on the belief that the 'problem' cannot be solved at local level. (3)

At the same time, a number of powers exist in the housing legislation which operate at local level. While the Housing Acts are not directly part of the planning machinery and, up to now, have mostly been implemented by professionals other than town-planners, the latter need to know how to handle the Housing Acts. It is hoped that in the future, local plans will incorporate such measures as are available in, say, a housing action area or a GIA, though recent moves by the DOE indicate that they see the powers as distinct. (4) Local authorities' housing strategies and investment programmes, for instance, do not necessarily relate to the planning process and do not undergo the process of public participation, though their influence on planning is obvious. (5) Similarly, the DOE has objected to statements of housing policies being included in local plans. The main points that it is relevant to consider here are the following: housing 'problem areas'; the various area-based treatments in the Housing Acts, and other kinds of area-based approaches; possible alternatives.

*Housing problem areas*
The origins of town-planning are to be found in nineteenth century housing and public health legislation. Not surprisingly, therefore, areas of 'bad' housing are so called principally on the basis of sanitary conditions: dampness, lack of bath, and overcrowding, for example.

Through time, a number of indices has been applied in various combinations and with different weights, to designate housing problem areas or stress areas. By choosing these indices and setting minimum standards, the problem is indirectly defined, whether this is perceived as such by the residents or not. (6)

More recently, additional non-physical measures have been introduced to try to make the identification of areas more closely related to actuality. Following the 1974 Housing Act, the DOE published *The use of indicators for area action*, which develops a methodology for defining various kinds of areas, using a number of indicators which include unemployment, incomes and proportion of pensioners. (7) Furthermore, various studies have gone beyond considering housing problems in isolation and have identified areas of 'multiple deprivation' or general stress: such areas were the concern of the Home Office's Community Development Projects, now discontinued. (8) It is worth referring here to a study undertaken in Merseyside between 1971 and 1973, in an area fictitiously called Luke Street, by Owen Gill. (9) Here, the construction in the 1930's of a number of large family houses and their occupation from the late 50's onwards by very large families, resulted in a problem area with inordinately high levels of delinquency. However, traditional 'housing stress' standards would probably not have picked this area as a difficult one, since the houses are owned by the local authority, in fair physical condition, not multi-occupied, not overcrowded, and with all amenities.
130

Having defined the problem and identified the areas where it is prevalent, local authorities have a number of powers to deal with it: traditionally, the way to solve housing problems of any kind was to demolish the buildings, with little regard to the consequences for the residents. At present, alternatives to blanket and massive redevelopment are at least considered, but in spite of pious advice from central government, the subsidy system until recently still tended to favour new housing rather than rehabilitation.

*Area-based treatments*
*Redevelopment and new development*: Under the Housing Act 1957, a local authority can purchase properties (compulsorily if necessary), demolish the existing buildings and erect new ones. (10) All residents of the area, at the time of the declaration, have to be rehoused before work on site starts; and at the end of the development, a totally new population will occupy the dwellings. Functions on the ground can be completely rearranged and, in theory, the new buildings will be of higher standard than the former ones and have a longer useful life. The local authority will have an almost abolute control over occupancy and the type and mix of residents, and the area may house more people than before (this is not always the case). Arguments in favour of redevelopment follow a number of criteria:

1 Condition of the dwellings and comparative costs of redevelopment as opposed to rehabilitation. In particular, if the local authority invokes Part III of the Housing Act, which deals with houses unfit for human habitation, redevelopment is the only solution.

2 Housing gain. Comparison between the number of people/households housed before and after redevelopment. Part V of the Housing Act deals with this aspect but includes also 'qualitative housing gain' which is more difficult to measure.

3 Local authority control is easier and more comprehensive in redevelopment than in any other form of housing action.

4 Ultimately, the desires of the existing residents should be a significant factor and it would be wrong to assume that they are always opposed to redevelopment. (11)

Local authorities often respond to tenants' complaints about new estates with the need to achieve a certain density, the housing cost yardstick, the lack of respect of tenants toward their environment, scarcity of funds, or some other scapegoat convenient at the time. Whilst all these may be partly justified, it may also be possible to look at new design solutions, adapting to modern needs the layouts of traditional housing which did achieve a higher level of satisfaction.

An example of such an attempt was put forward some years ago by Lionel March and Leslie Martin, and more recently by R MacCormac.

The proposal replaces the 'pavilion' type of development which is surrounded by a 'moat of indefensible space', by the 'court'. Provided that the developer is in control of a sufficiently large area, this type of 'ring' layout will allow for lower rise building, a higher level of flexibility and privacy, a greater feeling of spaciousness, and a better mix of land-uses, whilst keeping the desired density. The central open space could be occupied by the primary school, a shopping centre and/or recreation facilities and, with more elaborate designs, a higher percentage of private open space could be allocated to each dwelling. (12)

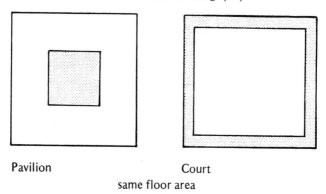

Pavilion         Court

same floor area

**Fig 22(a):** Two ways of utilising land. **Source:** R MacCormac, Housing form and land use, PTRC, 1974.

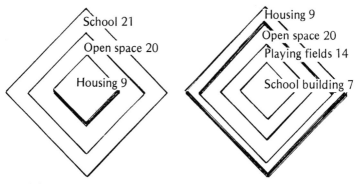

**Fig 22 (b):** The same example with specific allocations of land for various activities. **Source:** L Martin and L March, Urban Space and Structures, Cambridge, 1972.

*Improvement areas*: Incentives for improvement, and ways of obliging owners to improve their properties, have existed for a number of years under the Housing and Public Health Acts; and these have been, at times, moderately successful and, at other times, total failures. The 1969 Housing

Act introduced the General Improvement Areas. In spite of mixed results and a number of criticisms, these have been added to the other kind of areas introduced by the 1974 Housing Act. (13)

Originally, GIAs were areas where a local authority would concentrate its improvement efforts. Owners would have the security that no major redevelopment would take place, grants would be more readily available, and the local authority would show its confidence in the future by undertaking environmental improvements. The choice of the kind of area was crucial, but this was only realised later, after the unexpected effects were assessed. Where houses were tenanted, landlords either did nothing or, more often, got rid of their tenants and sold their property at vast profit to incoming owner-occupiers. The increase in land values, and the 'gentrification' of London's GIAs became political issues that almost killed the whole concept of area improvement.

Rather belatedly, central government issued circulars to advise on the kind of areas that should be selected for GIA treatment. They 'should be areas which offer scope for creating a better environment; and which contain stable communities largely free from housing stress. Districts with a preponderance of privately rented houses, especially furnished dwellings, will tend to be unsuitable for General Improvement treatment. (14) Additionally, authorities should ensure that the residents and owners would welcome the designation and would collaborate in its implementation. Since the 1974 Act, the kinds of grants given, and the proportion of the works covered by them, have been modified; table 4 shows how they are allocated in various kinds of areas. (15)

From a review of GIA reports, a few points need to be mentioned. Firstly, it appears that there has been confusion in the choice of priorities —is it housing or environmental improvement that is being pursued? Too often, efforts have concentrated on the latter, which should only be the means to achieve the former. Secondly, the residents' views are absolutely essential, since they will resent improvements that they did not want. Thirdly, implementation does not end with the planting of trees; they have to be watered and maintained as well. Finally, how is the success of a GIA to be measured? Presumably, by the improvement in the residents' housing conditions. This will be a valid yardstick, providing the old residents have not been replaced by new ones. (16)

*Housing action areas* As a consequence of the failure of the GIA's to solve the social problems of stress areas, the 1974 Housing Act introduced areas where action would be fast and concentrated. In housing action areas, local authorities not only can give grants at a higher level (see table 4) and undertake environmental improvements, but they also have powers of compulsory purchase to achieve objectives and to provide, improve, repair and manage housing accommodation. Additionally, landlords have to

| Type of grant | Purpose | Amount of eligible expense | Appropriate percentage | | |
|---|---|---|---|---|---|
| | | | HAA | GIA | Elsewhere |
| Improvement | Provision of Dwellings by Conversion or the Improvement of Dwellings beyond the provision of Standard Amenities | £2,000 or £2,400 for a dwelling provided by the conversion of a house or building of 3 or more storeys | 75 max. or 90 where proviso in S.59 | 60 max. | 50 max. |
| Intermediate | Provision of Standard Amenities where the Dwelling lacks any or all of them. | Up to £800 for repairs and replacements plus the cost of amenities | 75 or 90 where S.59 applies | 60 max. | 50 max. |
| | | | See Note 1 | See Note 1 | See Note 1 |
| Special | Provision of Standard Amenities in houses in multiple occupation. | Max. sums per amenity as laid down in S.70 and Schedule 6 | 75 max. or 90 where S.59 applies | 60 max. | 50 |
| Repair | Carrying out of works of repair or replacement to a dwelling, but only if it is in Housing Action Area or General Improvement Area, not being works linked with other works for conversion or improvement | Up to £800 | 75 max. or 90 where S.59 applies | 60 max. | Nil. |

*Note 1:* The Local Authority may fix a grant at a figure below the appropriate percentage for Improvement Grants, Special Grants and Repair Grants but must give reasons. They have no such discretion in relation to Intermediate Grants.

**Table 4: Summary of grants and grant conditions in housing action-areas, general improvement areas and elsewhere  (Source: Housing Act 1974)**

notify the local authority of any action they take in relation to ending a tenancy or disposing of their property. This will allow the authority to decide what measures to take in order to achieve the objectives for the area. (17)

In contrast with GIA's, HAA's should be areas of housing stress, with poor physical and social conditions These should be improved within a period of five years in order to secure:

a) the improvement of the accommodation in the area as a whole;

b) the well being of the persons living in the area;

c) the proper and effective management and use of that accommodation.

The period of five years can be extended for a further two with the Secretary of State's consent; but a limit has been imposed so that efforts are truly concentrated.

It is early to try to evaluate the results of HAA's, since only a limited number have been designated and none completed. In the past, all new kinds of action have had unexpected repercussions. One of them in the case of HAA's may be the eventual public monopoly of tenanted housing, with the resulting lack of choice for the non-owner-occupier citizen. Another, as with the GIA's, is the effect of action in one area on its surroundings. Finally, it would be wrong to expect yet again that housing measures can solve all social problems. (18)

*Priority neighbourhoods*: As a means of safeguarding areas adjacent to HAA's or GIA's from deteriorating as a result of action in those areas, the 1974 Housing Act introduced the 'priority neighbourhood' concept. Their characteristics are very similar to those of a HAA; they have at least one common boundary with a HAA or a GIA, but the circumstances must be such that it would not be practicable to designate them as HAA or GIA at this time. Powers in a priority neighbourhood are similar to those in a HAA, but grants for improvement are not a higher percentage of the works than in a non-designated area (see table 4). The duration for a priority neighbourhood is five years, and this can be extended for a further five years. Depending on the evolution of the priority neighbourhood and its adjacent areas, it can eventually be designated either as a GIA or a HAA. (19)

*Community development projects*: Up to now, we have discussed housing problems as if they can be isolated from other forms of deprivation. That this is not so was recognised by the government when it launched the Community Development Project in 1969—an experiment to deal with multiple deprivation on an area basis. The areas chosen were in very different parts of the country, some rural, some urban, and with varying characteristics. However, in most of them incomes were lower than

135

average, unemployment was high, and there was a high dependence on state benefits, plus poor health records and poor housing. (20)

A first conclusion of the CDP Inter-Project report in February 1974, was that the symptoms of disadvantage or social malaise could not be explained by personal failure of individuals (as the original scheme assumed), and that they were the result of external and structural deficiencies. (21) Just over a year later, another report by the CDP showed that the team had arrived at far reaching conclusions: 'The project's experience has led them largely to discount the value of attempting to influence policy and promote technical strategies for change in isolation from the development of working-class action. By this we do not mean vague schemes of 'participation' and 'involvement' in policy formation but rather the deliberate attempt to provide information and resources so that groups can formulate their own demands and press directly for change.' (22)

The team, therefore, predicted the failure of any scheme or experiment which assumed 'social pathology' linked to deprivation—such as the DOE Inner Area scheme or the DHSS Cycle of Deprivation Studies, which are mainly attempting a better coordination of services to improve the condition of the urban poor. However, the team had not completely abandoned an 'area-based' approach: 'The inter-project housing group came together initially to look at housing allocation policies and why ghetto estates had developed in project areas. The direction has now shifted towards the preparation of a critical analysis of the function of council housing, and the projects involved have now begun to chart in detail the history of post-war council housing to identify the causes and consequences of its decline.' (23)

The CDP's approach challenged the government's policies to deal with urban poverty at its roots, since it rejected partial 'aid' schemes as well as self-help ones. It also points out the highly policital character of planning, at any scale and regardless of the kind of issue considered. Finally, it is useful to remind ourselves that local problems may not always have local solutions.

*Possible alternatives*
More than a century of legislation has not solved the housing problem. Measures seem to be taken to try to correct previous errors which are exposed by the media and the experts. A short time goes by before the new measures are equally criticised and another set of proposals put forward. 'Nebulous objectives, decisions taken in response to "temporary crises", a multiplicity of different—and often unrelated—policies: these are the main features of "housing policy" in Britain today.' (24)

This is the rather depressing conclusion of a team of experts in housing research for CURS, Birmingham. Alternatives to the existing housing
136

system exist, and various authors have advocated a radical rethinking of housing policy. The theories of Colin Ward and other advocates of self-governance are worth mentioning since they have a particular relevance to local planning. (25)

All the existing legislation is based on the definition of minimum standards, and these standards are based on a societal consensus view of good management of a long-term communal asset—regardless of the wishes of the occupiers, who may be quite happy with the existing situation. The resident of a substandard dwelling—whether he knows it to be so or not—will sooner or later be rehoused or have his house improved—whether he wants it or not, or can afford it or not. This paternalistic approach ('We know what is good for you') and removal of choice quite naturally create resentment and apathy.

Co-operatives seem to be one of the ways in which the land ownership could be retained by the community, with the building and management of the housing put in the hands of the residents. There are great obstacles to developing housing co-operatives, both psychological and legal, but it is surprising that in the country where the co-operative movement was born so little progress and experimentation has taken place in the housing co-operative field. To be successful, standards would have to be relaxed and co-operatives allowed to decide for themselves what is best for them, with a minimum of supervision. The developments of the Lima 'barriadas' from shanty towns into solidly built neighbourhoods proves what can be done in far less favourable conditions. (26)  The experiments in Britain —by the London Borough of Haringey, or various schemes backed by the Housing Corporation—point in the right direction and could be emulated. (27)  Shankland, Cox and Partners' study on Lambeth, *Inner London: policies for dispersal and balance*, indicated the need to find alternative forms of tenure, and even to 'regularise' the situation of 'official squatters'. (28)

### Local planning and the housing problem
The previous paragraphs have treated the problems of housing at local level, but it has been hinted that there are wider implications. Two major questions are frequently discussed: is the problem of housing stress a local one or is it only the manifestation of a wider malaise? Is it possible to improve the housing situation by solving the problems of a particular locality?

The housing problem, as such, cannot be solved at the local level; but by improving conditions of a locality, some contribution is made at least to solving some of the problems.

It is probably fair to say that the housing problem will never be solved completely; aspirations change, people move, buildings deteriorate and society's resources are not unlimited. The chances are that positive action in one area will almost always have repercussions elsewhere, if only because resources spent in one place are thereby withheld from another. Additionally, by treating the problems on an area-base, individual cases outside the area—which may include a very large number of problem cases—will be ignored. There is certainly a case for trying to solve housing problems on an individual household, rather than an area, base; but this seems to be administratively impractical. (29)

However, the improvement of conditions in one area should not be considered as a negligible achievement, particularly if it can be done over a relatively short time. Old ladies living in damp basements have not the time to wait for an all-embracing solution to the housing problem; improvement of their own dwellings or their transfer to modern ones within their neighbourhood is what they may expect, and this should not be delayed for doctrinal reasons or because rehousing Mrs X means not rehousing Mrs Y. Priorities and needs have to be chosen on a pragmatically equitable basis, and action taken accordingly.

### Shopping

It is sometimes thought that action area planning means shopping centre renewal or redevelopment. This is partly due to the fact that central areas have triggered some of the early action area designations. Another reason is that, in time of economic growth, central area expansion seems the normal action to take, and both local authorities and developers are anxious to get on with it. In a no-growth situation, central area redevelopment projects are less likely to be implemented and, therefore, their preparation yields to more pressing matters, but the decline of a shopping area may well be a matter of urgent concern. (30)

While not trying to cover all aspects of the retailing activity, this section deals first with the changes in shopping habits and retail patterns that have taken place in the recent past, and their consequences at the local level.

*Changes in shopping habits and retail patterns*
Until about ten years after the end of the second world war, the pattern of distribution of shops was similar in most parts of the country—local corner shops in every village or neighbourhood, easily accessible to most local residents and offering a personal service which often included some form of credit; shopping parades and high streets with their local character, also offering personal services and owned by independent retailers, but including some chain stores or multiples; and the city centres where there was a concentration of services and department stores, surrounded by more multiples and independent shops. Mostly, this pattern resulted from the expansion of the cities during the nineteenth century and the concentration of retail outlets in the central areas, along the main roads and in the old residential areas, where front rooms were often converted

138

into shops. With the exception of the inter-war suburbs, where shopping development had often been neglected, the country as a whole was generously provided with shops covering the needs of every local area.

Authors vary in their opinions about what is the main reason for the changes that have occured in the past fifteen years or so, but they all agree that small and independent shops are declining in numbers, and that the character of high streets and city centres is changing towards greater uniformity and dominance by multiples and to the replacement of independent convenience shops by chain supermarkets. (31) The trend is bound to continue, as people who have for years managed a family shop retire and are not easily replaced in a demanding job with a low rate of return. The small shop suffers, also, because premises are old-fashioned and not easy to modernise; delivery services are inefficient and, therefore, not competitive; and, finally, because rents and taxes have risen considerably.

On the consumer side, a highly important factor has been the change in distribution of the population, mainly from the inner city to the outer suburbs. This has left the inner city small shops with a reduced clientele, generally with lower than average incomes. The upward mobile suburbanite in the meantime has changed his shopping habits and now relies on the motorcar for the once-a-week bulk-buying trip. The old high street with its lack of parking, narrow pavings, personal but slow service, and often higher prices, is abandoned for the out-of-town or edge-of-town purpose-built shopping centre, efficiently designed for the car-owning consumer.

The planner's and the developer's role has often ensured that small businesses were squeezed out. They have encouraged the concentration of shops in city centres, therefore killing smaller, weaker groups in the surrounding areas. Additionally, redevelopment schemes which aim at modernising facilities allow little place for the small independent trader, mainly because of the level of rents, and the character and functioning of these new centres.

It is worth considering in what sense and to what extent the decline of the small shop is a problem. It must be said that there was an over-provision of shops, justified mainly by the fact that it gave independent employment to a number of people willing to accept a low return for their work. These shops were often inefficiently run, made poor use of space, and compensated poor service by personal attention. High streets are not pleasant places in which to shop under present conditions, with traffic zooming through, bisecting them and polluting the environment. But this is not the whole story, as Ross Davies of the University of Newcastle states: 'However, the small local business, especially in the form of the corner shop, has increasingly come to be seen as more than just a business enterprise and to play a valuable social role for certain sections of the population within its immediate vicinity. It is a point of contact and sometimes a meeting place particularly for the elderly and children.' (32)

It is particularly in the inner city declining areas that the local shops have a role that transcends that of a retail outlet; and where their disappearance has caused most hardship. The old and less mobile members of the population suffer mostly, since they cannot reach the new retail centres, but at the same time they are the people who cannot afford the higher prices charged by those few remaining shops. In the suburbs, the same lack of corner shops is apparent, but since they never existed, they are less missed and residents are more used to travelling to the supermarket. Complaints have, however, been voiced; and the lack of local shops has been pointed out as one of the possible causes for the lack of community feeling in these areas.

On the high street, the problem is more complicated. The disappearance of the well known, independent shops that gave credit, sold small quantities and stayed open at odd hours, is seen as almost a personal loss by those to whom they were familiar. Even when the quality of shopping does not decline, the change of style is unwelcome. From the point of view of the environment, long high street frontages with empty premises or junk shops at the ends of them are an unfortunate consequence of the decline of the small shop. This blight tends to spread and often results in a complete change of character of the shopping area, sometimes giving it a new role. The interim period, where vacancies rise and dereliction spreads is detrimental to everybody. (33)

*Approaches to solutions*
Solutions vary from minor changes in the management of shops to total redevelopment. It is worth quoting Ross Davies once more: 'There is no question that the numbers of stores are too high and that substantial reductions have got to continue to occur. There will simply not be enough trade for them all to succeed.' (34)

It seems that the isolated corner shop may stay more easily than the independent ones located in a local shopping parade, but both may have to change their operations. A number of independent shopkeepers have entered voluntary trading groups, or have been helped by cash-and-carry operators who offer wholesale prices at lower levels than the traditional suppliers. (35)

In a paper delivered to the PTRC conference in July 1974, R K Schiller suggested that centres should, to a certain extent, specialise. Having observed that the biggest shopping magnets, the multiples, try to locate in the town centre whilst 'the high class and specialist retailer flees to the small town which the multiples scorn', he suggests turning this process on its head by building new centres of town and preserving the old centres as 'Latin Quarters for the city region'. (36) A compromise approach could be considered, whereby centres specialise and modernisation take place at
140

Fig 23: The first pedestrianized shopping street: London St, Norwich. By courtesy of Norwich City Council.

varying levels in different centres, some attracting the multiples, the others rejecting them. Taking, as an example, the Windsor town centre which has already been mentioned in this book, and its relation to Slough, Schiller says: 'Windsor, for example, has barely one-third the durable sales of Slough, yet it has more photographers, florists, jewellers, booksellers and antique shops than Slough.' (37)

This may still leave the 'Latin Quarter' residents without convenience shops. Examples of streets that have been taken over by the antiques trade are quite frequent; rents are pushed up till the greengrocer, dairy, baker and butcher are pushed out. London's Pimlico Road is a good example of this kind of transformation.

The planning approach should try to ensure the maintenance of essential services. One way this could be done would be through a change in the Use Class Order which would make the change from one kind of shop to another subject to planning application. The Association of Metropolitan Authorities, and the 'Save our local shops' campaign, suggested that 'shop' and 'local shop' should be two distinct categories. Until now, the DOE has been vaguely sympathetic, but little more (38) Other policies associated with this would be more flexibility in allowing shops to expand when they need to, and encouraging the provision of housing above shops (or the conversion of a ground-floor room into a shop) so that keeping longer hours is made easier for the shopkeeper.

In cases where the local authority is the owner or the developer of shopping premises, the first preoccupation should be the location of the units, which should try to maximise their catchment area. Instead of siting them at the centre of a housing estate, a location on the edge, or in a busy pedestrian route, or where cars can seen them and stop, would ensure them a certain amount of passing trade in addition to the local one.

Local authorities are not allowed to trade themselves, but they could support community shops, either through grants or by providing premises at minimum rents.

*Design considerations*
The first possibility is modernising old shopping streets in order to make them economically viable. To start with, the high street to be consolidated and improved should be carefully selected, possibly at the expense of other adjoining ones. Depending on the problems affecting it, the works will involve pedestrianising the street, or introducing some restrictions upon the automobile; the closure of some shops and a certain amount of redevelopment; the introduction of rear-access and parking facilities; the improvement of housing accommodation above and around the shops; and possibly the inclusion of community uses such as a library, a clinic or a public office. Improvements to the environment may also be considered, such as the planting of trees, provision of benches, new pavements, street

142

# TARUP CENTER

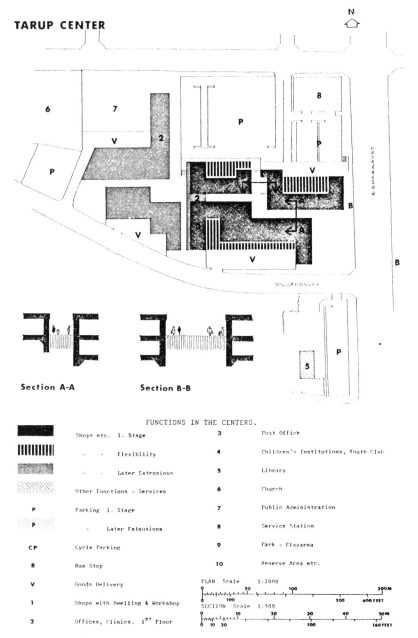

Section A-A          Section B-B

FUNCTIONS IN THE CENTERS.

| | | | |
|---|---|---|---|
| ▓▓▓ | Shops etc. 1. Stage | 3 | Post Office |
| ||||||| | " " Flexibility | 4 | Children's Institutions, Youth Club |
| ▒▒▒ | " " Later Extensions | 5 | Library |
| ▨▨▨ | Other Functions - Services | 6 | Church |
| P | Parking 1. Stage | 7 | Public Administration |
| P | " Later Extensions | 8 | Service Station |
| CP | Cycle Parking | 9 | Park - Playarea |
| B | Bus Stop | 10 | Reserve Area etc. |
| V | Goods Delivery | | |
| 1 | Shops with Dwelling & Workshop | | |
| 2 | Offices, Clinics. 1st Floor | | |

PLAN Scale    1:2000

SECTION Scale  1:500

Fig 24: Flexibility in the design of new shopping centres: Tarup, Denmark. Source: Institut for Center-Planlaegning, Denmark, 1968.

143

signs, etc. London Road in Norwich and the centre of Old Harlow are two of the best known examples of this kind of rehabilitation in England.

For new centres, a number of criteria have to be taken into account to help them in their success. Firstly, in the cases where a centre is part of a new housing estate or a new town neighbourhood, the phasing of shopping and residential development must be carefully coordinated; the centre cannot work at its full size right from the start, and the residents of the first completed houses cannot wait for years to get their shops. The design of the centre must, therefore, allow for growth and be functional at every stage of its development, reaching its full size only when the total population of the area has moved in. Flexibility has to be incorporated also to allow for changes even after the completion of the development. The Danish Institute for Center Planlaegning has shown how a number of small district centres in Denmark were developed with this kind of flexibility in mind. (39)

With regard to the design of new centres, the same recommendations as those put forward for the impovement of old ones apply. (40) If housing and/or employment uses are added, the centre will be more lively and utilised over a longer period of time during the course of a day. Two-tier centres are not entirely successful unless access from one level to the other is effortless and natural, or both levels lead to and from somewhere else. For instance, one level could be that of car access to the centre, and the other, that of pedestrian and public transport.

Protection from the weather is an added asset, but an arcade may be more pleasant as well as cheaper than a completely enclosed and air-conditioned centre. The combination of modern retail patterns with more traditional surroundings helps to make the customer feel at home in a new centre and may allow some independent shopkeepers to survive. For this, not only small units should be provided at low cost, but also the possibility of sub-standard or unconventional developments allowed—for instance, stalls or barrows should not automatically be chased out of a local centre and, in larger ones, a street market could be encouraged and so add to the popularity of the centre. The large enclosed developments, such as London's Brent Cross, are designed in such a way that no activity other than buying and selling in established shops can take place. In contrast, the more recently opened Brunel Centre in London seems to allow more flexibility, and provides a more lively atmosphere. The Covent Garden Market which will open in 1980 will also be an experiment in flexible letting and management policies.

### Environmental traffic management
The subject of this section is the impact of the motorcar on local areas —housing and shopping principally—and some possible solutions to the problems it generates.

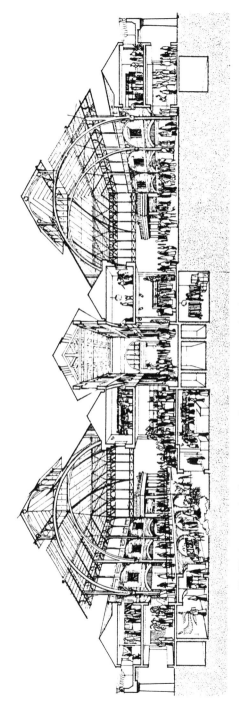

Fig 25: An example of a new approach to management of a shopping centre: the old Covent Garden Market converted. Source: GLC, Covent Garden Action Area Plan, 1978.

145

During the long and absolute reign of traffic engineers, traffic problems, such as congestion on certain routes, were dealt with by road widenings, road construction and realignments. The additional space created attracted more cars and, after a short-lived improvement, congestion arose again. Fortunately, in the last fifteen years (approximately), the folly of allowing the private car traffic to grow unrestrained has become apparent; and very diverse sectors of the community have started to react and campaign against it. In particular, they have shown the inequalities perpetuated by the private car and the negative effect it has on the environment.

By now, even the defenders of the motor car accept that measures have to be taken to reduce its impact. After the development of techniques to ease the flow of cars on particular roads—generally known as traffic management—a more recent concern has become that of environmental management. Schemes which are now traditional forms of design, such as the Radburn layout for residential areas, or pedestrian out-of-town shopping centres, were already conceived with this environmental quality in mind. (41) All measures related to environmental management involve some degree of traffic restraint, ie reduce the possibility of using the motor car with total impunity. The reasons for introducing environmental traffic management measures vary from reducing pollution to avoiding accidents; from increasing pedestrian comfort, to improving bus reliability.

In 1963, Colin Buchanan's report *Traffic in towns* introduced the concept of 'environmental areas': 'an area having no extraneous traffic, and within which considerations of environment predominate over the use of vehicles.' (42) The report also showed that traffic and land-use are two inseparable functions. 'They (vehicles) move only because people want them to move in connexion with activities which their drivers are engaged in.' Finally, the report showed the relation between three variables: accessibility, environment and cost, and how the modification of one would affect the other two. For instance, if cost is fixed, an improvement of accessibility can only be achieved by a deterioration of the environment. (43)

*Criteria*
The three characteristics to be recorded are the traffic itself, the main activities and the physical layout of the area.

*Traffic*: The kind of information that needs to be gathered includes the flow of traffic—generally obtained through vehicle counts at specific times; the proportion of through to local traffic; the nature and kind of vehicles, eg private cars, congestion or bottlenecks, dangerous junctions and points of conflict. The negative effects on the pedestrian can be measured by accidents, delays experienced by people wishing to cross a road; the ease or difficulty of access to various land-uses; the congestion of
146

footways, or the difficulties of engaging in any activity, such as talking, on them. Specific factors can be of greater importance due to the degree of sensitivity of a particular use: in the vicinity of a school, for instance, safety becomes a high priority and the tolerable capacity of the roads may have to be lowered in comparison with other areas. (44)

*Land-uses*: Existing and potential land-uses are a basic factor which have to be considered in all cases. The sensitivity of specific activities to the impact of traffic, their demand for parking and the amount of traffic they generate—whether pedestrian, motor, commercial, private or public—needs recording.

Residential areas are particularly sensitive because of the risks to children and because of noise, dirt and fumes pollution, visual intrusion and vibration. At the same time, people like to have their own cars near at hand and in a secure place; they like to be able to unload groceries at the door and to see their car from the window. The problem is, however, relatively simple to measure in that, with the exception of occasional deliveries or emergency vehicles, there is only one kind of traffic generated by these areas—that of the residents themselves or their visitors. All other traffic is extraneous, and one of the goals of the exercise should be to keep it out.

The problem is more complicated in shopping areas; particularly since, for historical reasons, most existing shopping streets are also major through-routes. Conflict arises because of the various kinds of traffic competing for space on the roads—the vehicles making deliveries to shops, the car-owning shopper arriving or leaving the place, the same parking, the pedestrian shopper, public transport, through traffic and that generated by other local uses, residential, commercial, etc. Oxford Street in London, one of the more complex shopping streets in the country, has numerous traffic problems even after the implementation of a number of restraint measures. (45) Since the objectives of various users may clash, it is particularly important to determine what they are and what priorities should be accepted; there is, however, a substantial amount of evidence to show that, if sensitively designed, environmental traffic management schemes can in fact increase sales. Norwich's London Street is one of the best known examples where this has happened. (46)

*Layout*: The third element to be recorded, apart from land-uses and traffic characteristics, is the layout of streets or, more generally, the traffic infrastructure of the area, which will determine the capacity of the roads. Junctions, footpaths, traffic-lights, pedestrian crossings, bridges, under-passes or tunnels, bus lanes, bus stops and lay-bys, are important; as well as restrictions indicated by signs such as no parking, one way streets, and limitations to turning left or right. Existing restrictions and traffic characteristics may sometimes result in 'rat-runs', where to avoid congested main roads, cars may cut through narrow residential streets and have detrimental effects on the environment. It is also important to record the characteristics

147

of the roads surrounding the study area, since any action taken in it is bound to have ripple effects which will, at least, have to be monitored. Finally, the relationship between the roads and the buildings can be important—parking on or off street, access to service areas, forecourts or garages, servicing or restrictions to it.

The physical characteristics of the area, together with the dominant land-uses, will give an indication of the environmental capacity of the area. This Buchanan has defined as 'the capacity. . .to accommodate moving and stationary vehicles, having regard to the need to maintain the environmental standards', and these in turn are 'a state of affairs defined as acceptable in relation to any or all of the direct or indirect effects of motor traffic on the environment' (47)

Finally, a quote from the Barnsley town centre draft action area plan: 'The Town Centre functions depend to a large degree for their success on a transport system which strikes the right balance between the needs of the various users. Policies are required for traffic and pedestrian movement to resolve conflicts and achieve a satisfactory system for movement in the Town Centre.' (48)

*Design*

Any measure to regulate traffic is a form of environmental traffic management, even the requirement that motorists drive on the left or right side of the road. To quote the Windsor town centre draft plan: 'Traffic management measures can lessen the detrimental effects of vehicles on the environment while retaining convenient access for essential traffic.' (49)

In the process of designing an environmental traffic management scheme, it is essential to test every step being taken, to ensure that it does not have unforeseen and negative consequences. One of the most widely used measures is to exclude extraneous traffic from a particular area, but if accessibility is to be maintained, the area's peripheral roads have to be able to carry the traffic thus diverted without detrimental consequences for those living on the periphery or in the adjacent areas. After implementing a part of their environmental traffic management scheme for Barnsbury, Islington borough council undertook a review of its functioning. It found that on the basis of a number of criteria (safety, noise, vibration, pollution, etc) conditions within the area had improved; but on the periphery, they had deteriorated: 'We consider that in terms of the changes that have taken place, in the direct benefits and the direct disbenefits, the position is roughly equal.' (50)

Once the distributory network peripheral to the area has been chosen, design can start within the area to ensure good environmental conditions as well as accessibility to the various buildings or sites. One of the principal forms of avoiding penetration by through traffic and rat-runs, is to reduce the number of entry-points from the peripheral roads into the area;
148

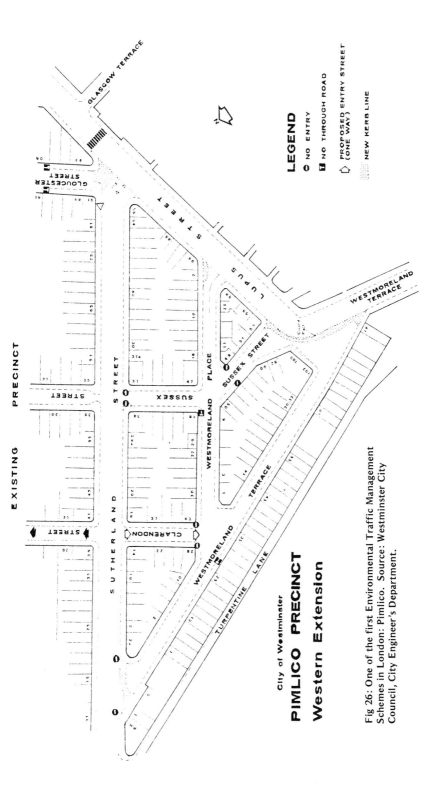

City of Westminster

# PIMLICO PRECINCT
## Western Extension

Fig 26: One of the first Environmental Traffic Management Schemes in London: Pimlico. Source: Westminster City Council, City Engineer's Department.

LEGEND

○ NO ENTRY

▣ NO THROUGH ROAD

⬆ PROPOSED ENTRY STREET (ONE WAY)

░ NEW KERB LINE

EXISTING PRECINCT

GLASGOW TERRACE

GLOUCESTER STREET

LUPUS STREET

SUSSEX STREET

WESTMORELAND PLACE

WESTMORELAND STREET

WESTMORELAND TERRACE

SUTHERLAND STREET

CLARENDON STREET

TURPENTINE LANE

exit-points need not be reduced to the same extent, but the fewer access-points to or from the distributors, the higher their capacity will be. There should be no easy route through the area, so that even if a car entered the area, it would be discouraged from using its streets as a short cut. Both the Barnsbury and the Pimlico schemes are based on this approach. (51) Additional measures can be taken, such as the narrowing of the carriage-way at entry- and exit-points, or the limiting of access to certain vehicles and/or to certain times of the day. Additionally, speed controls can be achieved by sleeping policemen, increased safety for the pedestrian and the motorist through redesigned junctions, rearranging parking, no entry signs, pedestrian-controlled traffic lights and crossings, etc. (52) Play streets have been introduced in some residential areas where only local cars are allowed and children can play in relative safety. In shopping areas, simple measures may include the widening of footpaths, the rearrangement of crossing points, the building of subways or bridges, parking and waiting restrictions, the rearrangement of shop access, etc. More fundamental measures include the banning of certain kinds of traffic (as in Oxford Street), rearrangement of servicing and deliveries, and partial or total pedestrianisation. This is not always the best solution, and the cost of achieving it is not always justified. As Jane Jacobs said: 'To think of city traffic in over-simplified terms of pedestrians versus cars and to fix on the segregation of each as a principal goal, is to go to the problem from the wrong end. Consideration for pedestrians in cities is inseparable from consideration for city diversity, vitality and concentration of use.' (53)

Unless there is a substantial level of activity in the street at all times, a large car-free area can become bleak, desolate and even dangerous to pedestrians, and a certain level of motor traffic can provide useful policing. Additionally, these traffic-free zones are often surrounded by an almost insurmountable ring-road or a sea of parking, turning them into islands only linked to the rest of the world through bridges and underpasses.

Finally, the level of parking provision can regulate the flow of traffic in an area. Thus, in a residential area, the amount of kerbside space available for parking is limited; off-street space may or may not be available. If extraneous traffic is to be kept out—particularly when the housing is near a commercial area—on-street parking must be restricted for commuters, but allowed for residents. In inner London, this has been achieved by selling special permits which allow residents to park in certain areas reserved for them on the street, whilst all other cars have to park on meters which are much more expensive. In other areas, different priorities may have to be established between long-term users (commuters), short-term ones (shoppers) and those on business. In shopping centres it may be difficult or very expensive to provide adequate parking. One of the reasons for the decline of the inner city shopping district is that it cannot provide as much convenience in terms of parking as the out-of-town or suburban

150

centre built with the car in mind. For this reason, many retailers in the USA offer to refund the cost of parking to any shopper who spends above a certain sum in their shops; other stores provide their own parking facilities.

But it must be added that banning or severely restricting access to an area by private car can only be done if it is allied with an efficient, reliable and flexible public transport system.

## Three examples

The three examples which are described as a conclusion to this section share a certain number of characteristics. None is in Britain (one is in Argentina and two in the USA); the three are in environments where the private car has a very dominant role, but in these particular cases it has been severely restricted; the dominant land-use is non-residential—in one example it is shopping, in the other two, entertainment. There the similarities end.

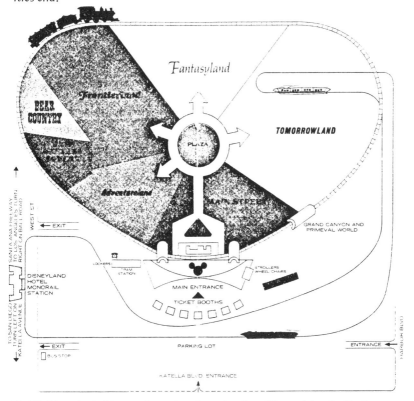

Fig 27: Disneyland: 74 acres devoted to the pedestrian with a variety of collective transportation systems.

151

'Enter a different world—Disneyland', says the sign over the ticket office, and once the visitor has been through the gates and into the vast recreation centre in California, he knows how true this statement is— though not necessarily only for the reasons thought up by the Walt Disney company. In a city-region where you can be arrested for walking, and where public transport is nearly non-existent, here is an area of forty-three acres where no private cars are allowed. The grounds are given over to the pedestrian, and to functioning models of a variety of public transport systems, buses, monorail, railway, paddlesteamer, horse -drawn streetcars, etc. The two rail systems not only circulate within the fair, but also link it with some of the facilities on the periphery, mainly, a hotel and the gigantic parking-lot which surrounds Disneyland and which is the price that has to be paid for the absence of cars inside. Within the area, thousands of people mill around, obviously attracted by the entertainment facilities available, but possibly also by the novelty of using their legs. The internal layout is simple, and the routes follow the desired lines. The public transport vehicles are used to capacity almost constantly, and they are not free.

Also in the car-obsessed state of California, Yosemite National Park covers some 1,189 square miles of mountains, forests and lakes. One road crosses the park from east to west, and a loop road takes visitors from the west side of the park to Yosemite Village and back along the banks of the Merced River. Around this area are some of the main attractions of the park, including the giant sequoia trees and superb waterfalls. However, cars are not allowed to go beyond the main road in Yosemite Valley. The sites can be reached on foot or bicycle, or by a bus service which 'operates the year-round and is free, fun and frequent'. Its cost is covered by the right of entry to the park. The main advantage of this system is that even during the peak holiday season, the park, though full, is not crowded, and its natural features are protected from the litter and pollution that would be generated by the same number of people driving their cars. Less than one-third of a mile from the parking places, the sites are virtually unspoilt though still easily accessible.

The third example is a traditional shopping street in Buenos Aires, the capital of Argentina, and a city of over eight million inhabitants. Florida Street has been the main shopping street for generations a cross between Oxford Street and Bond Street, though more like the latter in scale. It is about a mile in length and, being part of the grid-iron layout of the city, it is interrupted every 100 metres by cross-streets. Along it are a multiplicity of shops selling durables, cafés, restaurants, banks, travel agents, a few hotels, a number of arcades and offices above most of these. It is the only street outside London's Brompton Road that boasts a Harrods department store. However, the main attraction of Florida Street is that it is totally pedestrianised and is, therefore, full of people almost
152

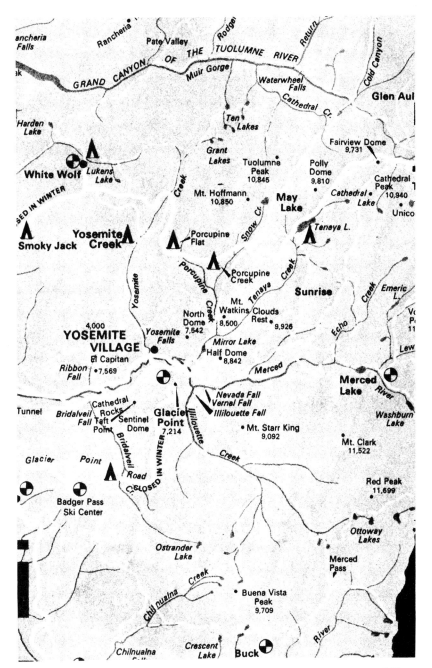

Fig 28: Yosemite Park, USA.

153

Fig 29: Florida Street in Buenos Aires: a mile of pedestrian shopping.

154

twenty-four hours a day. It has been more or less so for over thirty years. Until the early 1970's, cars were allowed from 1am to 10am, when deliveries took place. More recently, the pavement has been raised to the level of the footpath, kiosks and troughs for plants installed and cars are now banned at all times. Since they are allowed on the cross-streets, deliveries have to take place from these, either on foot or with trolleys. Buses circulate along the cross-streets and the two parallel streets, a hundred metres away. The success of this scheme is undisputed; people having business in the central area almost always walk through Florida Street even if it means making a detour, because its environment is so much more pleasant than anywhere else in town.

These three examples are given here because they are unconventional by British standards, and cover environmental traffic schemes on a scale comparable to that of a local plan. While it is recognised that they cannot be copied in different situations, their boldness may be a source of inspiration.

## Recreational areas

For years, social scientists have been announcing the advent of a new era, that of the 'leisure society', in which machines would do most of the work and humans would have, at last, time for leisure. Until now, reality has been quite different, but compared with fifty years ago, the amount of time available for leisure during part of the day, weekend and annual holidays, is significantly more; and substantial investment has taken place at all levels of the recreation market, from private and public funds, turning it into an important industry in its own right.

### Supply and demand for facilities

Some local authorities still assume that all they have to do about recreation is to provide x number of acres of open space per 1000 inhabitants. At the same time, a number of studies has shown that the people's choice of recreation pursuits varies with age, income, education, car-ownership, etc, and generalisations cannot usefully be made. (54)

The official attitudes of the past have had a number of negative effects. By being paternalistic, they discouraged active participation by the public who, therefore, accepted what was given to them and used it if it coincided with their desires; if not, they ignored it without getting a valid replacement. This tended to reinforce patterns, particularly those related to income and education, and to perpetuate prejudices.

To a great extent, demand for recreation facilities can be affected by the supply, very much as happens with other commodities. Until a swimming pool is built in an area, people will not necessarily express the desire to swim, but this will grow as soon as the facility is provided. There seem to be various ways of estimating demand for recreation, based

155

| Type | Main function | Approximate Size | Distance from home | Characteristics |
| --- | --- | --- | --- | --- |
| (a) Metropolitan Park | Weekend and occasional visits by car or public transport | 150 acres | 2 miles, or more where the park is appreciably larger | Either (i) natural heathland, downland, commons, woodlands, etc, or (ii) formal parks providing for both active and passive recreation, eg boating, entertainments, etc. May contain playing fields but at least 100 acres for other pursuits. Adequate car parking essential. |
| (b) District Park | Weekend and occasional visits on foot | 50 acres | 3/4 mile | Containing playing fields, but at least 30 acres for other pursuits (as in local parks) and some car parking |
| (c) Local Park | For pedestrian visitors including nearby workers | 5 acres | 1/4 mile | Providing for court games, children's play, sitting-out areas, landscaped environment, and playing fields if the parks are large enough |
| (d) Small Local Park | Pedestrian visits especially by old people, children, and workers at midday; particularly valuable in high density areas | Under 5 acres | 1/4 mile or less | Gardens, sitting-out areas and/or children's playgrounds |

**Table 5: GLDP guidelines on public open space**

either on established standards and demographic analysis of the population (eg x number of football pitches per 1000 of males between the ages of y and z), or based on observation and interviewing (eg asking people what kind of facility they would like, and how they use what is offered, plus observing their habits). Additionally, social scientists may suggest needs based on theoretical hypotheses about human behaviour. These have not been very successful up to now: 'Although a great deal of empirical research has been conducted, much urban leisure policy is based on assumptions which are at best unsubstantiated or at worst definitively disproved. The normative reformist spirit which has enveloped public recreation policy could have something to do with this.' (55)

If the often-quoted standard of seven acres of open space per 1000 population that is accepted as the only standard to measure the supply for recreation, some urban areas in Britain are far from reaching it and are very deprived indeed. The London Borough of Islington had, until recently, less than one acre per 1000 population and was the worst off local authority in the country. (56) It is, however, worth asking whether a magic figure (for which hundreds of dwellings would have to be demolished) would be the best way of benefiting the residents. The questions to be asked are, what are the main recreational groups and what are their needs? How are their demands expressed? What are the best ways of satisfying them? The answers to these questions are in such studies as Thomas Burton's *Recreation research and planning*, the above-quoted RTPI publication *Leisure in the urban environment*, and Ben Whitaker and Kenneth Browning's *Parks for people* (57)

*Provision and design*
The satisfaction of demands for recreation is particularly difficult to achieve, because the demands are not always clearly expressed, they can vary over a relatively short time, and the priority given to them in public sector's budgets is low. Therefore the facilities must be carefully selected, provide as much flexibility as possible and be used as intensively as possible. A few examples and comments will be enough to indicate what can be done.

*Open air facilities*
In a local area, open space will probably be scant, from the play area for toddlers, to the local park of a maximum of, say, five acres. Therefore, one principle to be followed is that variety should be aimed at, both in terms of activities and forms. Landscaping, eg hedges, trees and changes in level, can provide variety as well as separating the open space from other uses and baffling the noise of traffic; it can also permit various activities to take place at the same time without interfering with each other. This can also be achieved by having a number of small open spaces, each one with

157

Fig 30: Local authority's ideas of recreation areas.

Fig 31: A vest-pocket park in Manhattan (Paley Park). An oasis in the middle of the frantic city.

a special function, rather than one large one. Skilful use of different ground textures (grass, paving slabs, cobblestones, flower beds, etc) can also offer variety, and direct people's movements without the need of 'prohibition' signs.

Two examples are mentioned here. Both are on very small sites, located in busy city centres and successful in terms of offering people relief from their urban environment during working hours. The first is in the heart of Manhattan—Paley Park, only 42 x 100ft, a square between tall buildings and a busy street. A few steps lead up to it and in it are a few trees, tables and seats and waste bins. The side walls are exposed brick, the ground is cobbled and near the entry there is a sandwich store. But the main attraction is the back wall, 20ft high, covered with a waterfall which cools the air during the summer, and the noise of which totally isolates the place from the traffic.

The second example is a recently laid out open space in Covent Garden, on ground owned by the Arts Council and reserved for future expansion of the Royal Opera House. It is about 50 metres square, but looks much larger, partly because it is surrounded by cleared space and the central market hall. Laid out with a Silver Jubilee grant, it has different levels,

159

varied vegetation, a brick floor, sitting areas and a mock ruined temple.

The latter example illustrates another important point in the design of open space—people's involvement in it. Covent Garden's 'pocket park' (as these are called in the USA) was the third effort of a group of local people who formed an 'open spaces committee' to try to obtain the use of land awaiting development for more than eighteen months. They managed to get top-soil, plants and paving materials, and to mobilise local muscle power to dig and plant. The first of these gardens disappeared after about two years; the Japanese water garden, as it was known, was a success mainly because it was the result of collective local effort. People felt it was theirs and not a municipal imposition. Children were given a tree or a shrub to plant and they were responsible for it; vandalism was therefore minimal since they acted as vigilantes and would not let other kids destroy them. Adventure playgrounds, similarly, stimulate children's imaginations, allow them to do what they like, constructively or destructively, and do not consume much land. Because they can be unsightly or displease some members of the community, they are best shielded from view and they need to be supervised.

Local authorities' housing schemes often have a substantial amount of non-usable open space. 'Amenity open spaces', are they are known in local government jargon, if handed over to the tenants could vary from allotments to ball-playing areas, and from sitting-out spaces to adventure play-grounds.

'Joint involvement in the running of open spaces can contribute with a sense of territory—to a feeling of community. Although it is the lower income groups with fewer private gardens and less chance of visiting the country who have the most urgent need of parks, open spaces can provide experience of community co-operation for all types of neighbourhood.' (58)

*Indoor facilities*
It is another reflection of the Victorian heritage that public authorities have devoted their energy in terms of recreation almost exclusively to open spaces. A number of social problems can probably, at least in part, be attributed to a lack of indoor facilities. It is, therefore, comforting to read in the recently published Wandsworth town centre draft plan: 'In the short term it is possible to use a ground floor flat for under five year olds to meet some of the immediate needs of young children in Wandsworth Plain Estate, especially over the school holiday period'. (58)

Local needs can appear so extensive that nothing is done by the local authority until it can find a perfect solution for all of them. However, rather than wait for the land and the funds to build a swimming pool, it may be better to use an empty shop or building to provide play facilities, a crèche, a workshop or a rehearsal room. Neither the building nor the facility need to be permanent and there is hardly any area where vacant

160

premises do not exist, awaiting either demolition, change of use or simply a decision. Little needs to be invested by public authorities; local skills and goodwill can turn an empty building into a useful asset for the community. As in the case of open spaces, people's involvement in the project assures that it will be looked after and will be used. (60)

The following proposals are found in the already mentioned Wandsworth town centre plan:

1 The provision of a community centre in converted premises on the Convent Site, West Hill by 1980.

2 The old Country Court House, Garratt Lane, which is now in temporary use by the Arndale Centre Tenants play group and the Adult Education Institute, which runs a family craft-work shop to serve the local area.

3 The old Co-op shop in Wandsworth High Street will be used with the council's help, as a local artists' workshop. (61)

In the same context, the following policies in the Covent Garden plan are welcome:

'The design and realisation of open space will be carried out with the close participation of local people.'

'The opportunity should be taken, where possible, to use temporarily vacant sites and unoccupied buildings for recreation purposes.' (62)

The best opportunity for the provision of recreation facilities both indoors and outdoors is given by the local schools. These are generally well equipped for sports, cultural and technical pursuits, and are only in use during part of the day and part of the year. With the reduction in schools enrolment and rationalisation of schools use, a number of sites is becoming redundant and offers new opportunities for recreational facilities. More control of what happens in them could be given to the local community.

Other institutions through which more recreation facilities could be made available are the churches, which control a substantial amount of land and buildings. Traditionally, they have always been involved in recreation, but a renewed effort could be of great help in deprived areas. If the church premises themselves are redundant, the buildings can often be converted to a number of uses for both social and sporting activities.

## REFERENCES

1 See for instance D C Stafford, *The economics of housing policy*, Croom Helm, London, 1978.

2 Central Housing Advisory Committee, 'Houses for today and tomorrow', the Parker Morris Report, HMSO, London, 1961.

3   There are, however, a number of excellent and fundamental texts on housing, such as: A Murie, P Niner and C Watson, *Housing policy and the housing system*, George Allen & Unwin, London, 1976.  D V Donnison, *The government of housing*, Penguin Books, London, 1967. *Council housing: purposes, procedures and priorities, ninth report of the Housing Management Sub-Committee*, HMSO, London, 1969.

4   Department of the Environment, Local Plans Note 1/78, Form and Content of Local Plans, paras 16 and 17.

5   The Housing Strategies and Investment Programmes were introduced by a Government Green Paper in 1976 and then included in Circulars 18/77, Housing Capital Expenditure and 63/77, Housing Strategies and Investment Programmes.

6   See, for instance, Housing Act 1957, c56, Part II, S4 as amended by Housing Act 1969, Part VI, S71, for definition of matters to be taken into account to determine whether a house is unfit for human habitation.

7   DOE, The use of indicators for area action, Housing Act 1974, Area Improvement Note 10, HMSO, 1975.

8   National Community Development Project, Interim Project Report, 1973 and Forward Plan, 1975.  For area management, see also T Mason, K Spencer, C Vielba and B Webster, *Tackling urban deprivation: the contribution of area-based management*, University of Birmingham, 1977.

9   O Gill, *Luke Street—housing policy, conflict and the creation of the delinquent area*, Macmillan Press, London, 1977.

10   Housing Act 1957, c56, part II, S43.

11   For reactions to Local Authorities' new developments, see for instance DOE, Development Directorate, 'High density housing', Housing Development Paper 1/73, reprinted from *Architect's journal* Jan 3 1973. DOE, Development Directorate, 'Local authority housing', Paper 2/73, reprinted from *Architect's journal* August 1 1973. DOE, Design Bulletin 25, *The estate outside the dwelling*, HMSO, London, 1972. DOE, Design Bulletin 21, *Families living at high density*, HMSO, London, 1970. See also, J R Mellor, *Urban sociology in an urbanized society*, Routledge & Kegan Paul, London, 1977, pp98-107, for a general explanation of high rise dwelling.

12   L Martin and L March (eds), *Urban space and structures*, Cambridge University Press, 1972, Part 1, 'Explorations'.  R MacCormac, 'Housing form and land use', in *Proceedings of seminar G, housing*, PTRC Summer Annual Meeting, University of Warwick, July 1974, pp67-86.

13   Housing Act 1969, c33, Part II, General Improvement Areas and Housing Act 1974, c44, Part V, General Improvement Areas and Schedule 5.

14   DOE Circular 13/75, Housing Act 1974 Renewal Strategies, para. 18. See also DOE Circular 14/75, Housing Act 1974: Parts IV, V and VI.

15   Housing Act 1974, Part V, General Improvement Areas; Part VII on grants and Circular 14/75, Memorandum C.

16   For further reading on GIA's, see J T Roberts, *General improvement areas*, Saxon House, 1976; and M Hanson, 'When will GIAs work?' in *Municipal and public services journal*, Oct 26 1973, pp1592-1601.

17   Housing Act 1974, c44, Part IV and DOE Circular 14/75, Memorandum A.

18   For further reading on HAAs, see for instance 'Housing Action Areas', in the *Guardian* Jan 15 1976, 8 (2) and 'Colville-Tavistock: the first Housing Action Area', in *Architect's journal*, July 16 1975, pp114-116.

19   Housing Act 1974, c44, Part VI and Circular 14/75, Memorandum B.

20   CDP Information and Intelligence Unit, Inter-Project Report 1973, published in 1974.

21   CDP, op cit, para 3.12, p8 and section 4, Action and Research Strategies, pp23-27.

22   CDP Information and Intelligence Unit, The National Community Development Project, Forward Plan 1975—76, p1.

23   CDP, Forward Plan, p4.

24   A Murie, P Niner and C Watson, op cit, chapter 9, p248.

25   C Ward, *Housing: an anarchist approach*, Freedom Press, London, 1976.

26   J Turner, *Housing by people*, M Boyars, London, 1976.

27   For further reading on co-operatives, see for instance: J Hands, 'Housing co-operatives and the inner-cities', paper given at the Polytechnic of the South Bank National Conference—Homes and Jobs in Inner Cities, Sept 1977, vol 2. G Meehan, 'Homes for Haringey', in *Haringey star*, May 1976. R Hackney, 'Black Road—self-help in Macclesfield', in *Housing review* 24 (5), Sept/Oct 1975, pp130-131. Publications by the Co-operative Housing Agency of the Housing Corporation.

28   Shankland, Cox and Partners, op cit, in particular chapter 8, pp162-163.

29   See also Council Housing: Purposes, Procedures and Priorities, op cit and Building Research Station, Open Days 17-14 Sept 1975, particularly Paper OD 4b.

30   Indeed, a number of local plans that have been produced and those quoted here, were town centres, eg Windsor, Richmond, Wandsworth town centres.

31   R Davies, 'The recent history and problems of small shops and related small business', in Jones and Oliphant (Eds), *Local shops: problems and prospects*, Unit for Retail Planning Information, Reading, 1976.

32   R Davies, op cit, p18.

33   See for instance City of Westminster, Development Plan—Report on Stage One: Problems, Issues and Priorities, Oct 1974, paras 1.126—

1.128 pp53 and 54. Also London Borough of Wandsworth, Shopping Policy Review, Borough Plan No 2, 1977, p11, paras 45-50; and London Borough of Lambeth, Lambeth Development Plan, Policy Discussion Paper, 1978, The pattern of shopping in Lambeth, p3 (2).

34   R Davies, op cit, p18.

35   D H Lingham and J G A Irish, 'Voluntary trading groups and cash and carry as a means of support for small shops', in Jones and Oliphant, op cit, pp81-85. See also R Davies, op cit.

36   R K Schiller, 'Retailing and planning—A commercial viewpoint', in *Retailing and local planning*, proceedings of seminar F, Summer Annual Meeting, PTRC, University of Warwick, July 1974, p46.

37   R K Schiller, op cit, p46.

38   A Brown, 'Small shops in jeopardy' in *Planning* March 18 1977, pp8-9. And also *Planning* May 27 1977, p6: 'Shop use class clause quashed'; reporting the House of Lords refusal to allow the London Borough of Kensington and Chelsea to restrict the freedom of changing use within the shopping category.

39   Institute of Center Planlaegning, *Shopping centres—planning for changes and flexibility*, Seven Danish Examples, Lyngby, 1968.

40   R Davies, 'Planning solutions to the problems of the small shop', in *Town & country planning*, vol 44, no 4, April 1976, pp215-220.

41   The Radburn principle was introduced by Clarence Stein and Henry Wright in their plan for Radburn, New Jersey in 1928. See Toward New Towns for America, C Stein, Liverpool University Press, 1958.

42   *Traffic in towns*, The specially shortened edition of the Buchanan Report, Penguin Books, 1964, glossary, p252.

43   *Traffic in towns*, p45 and pp66 and 67.

44   For the impact of traffic, see London Borough of Richmond upon Thames, An Environmental Assessment of the Proposed Richmond Town Centre Traffic Management Scheme, April 1976. See also L Cohen, 'Use of indices to evaluate the effect of traffic management schemes on the environment', paper given at the Polytechnic of the South Bank, during a three-day course on 'Techniques and local planning' 19-21 Sept 1978.

45   J Parker and C Hoile, 'Central London's pedestrian streets and ways', in *Greater London intelligence quarterly*, no 33, Dec 1975, pp16-27. J Parker and J Eburah, 'Oxford Street experiment: bus and environmental improvement scheme', *Greater London intelligence quarterly* no 25, Dec 1973, pp13-19. T Aldous, 'Furnishing the exterior environment' in *Built environment*, Vol 3, no 6, June 1974, pp292-295.

46   A A Wood, *Norwich the creation of a foot street*, Norwich City Council Planning Dept, 1969. And also J Antoniou, *Environmental management, planning for traffic*, McGraw-Hill, 1971, p57.

47   *Traffic in towns*, glossary, p252.

48   Barnsley Metropolitan Borough Council, Barnsley Town Centre Draft Action Area Plan, February 1978, para 2.7 32, p42.

49   Royal Borough of Windsor and Maidenhead, Windsor Town Centre District Plan, Aug 1977, para 11.2.4 p52.

50   Islington Borough Council, Barnsbury Environmental Traffic Management Report, Report of the Traffic Management Working Party, para 3.81, p81. See also L Cohen, op cit.

51   City of Westminster, City Engineer's Department, Pimlico Precinct Traffic Scheme, Oct 1968.

52   A Miller, *Radburn and its validity today*, Building Research Station, Current Paper 36/39, 1969.

53   J Jacobs, *Death and life of great American cities*, Penguin Books, 1972, p362.

54   D D Molyneux, 'A framework for recreational research', in T L Burton (ed) *Recreation research and planning*, George Allen & Unwin, London, 1970, chapter 2, pp47-62.

55   N Perry, 'Social theory and urban leisure' in the Royal Town Planning Institute's *Urban crisis, leisure in the urban environment*, 1976, p18.

56   Islington Borough Council, Islington Borough Development Plan, Report of Studies, Topic Paper No 3, Recreational Open Space, Aug 1972, chapter 6, Assessment of need and deficiency, pp65-84.

57   T L Burton (ed) op cit, particularly chapters 2 and 12. B Whitaker and K Browning, *Parks for people*, Seeley, Service & Co, London, 1971.

58   B Whitaker and K Browning, op cit, p34.

59   London Borough of Wandsworth, Wandsworth Town Centre Plan, July 1977, para 63, p14.

60   Greater London Council, The Greater London Council (Covent Garden) GLC Action Area Plan, London 1978, p37, para B.10.4 and para B.10.16, p38. The Jubilee Hall is an ex-market warehouse on the South side of the Covent Garden piazza.

61   London Borough of Wandsworth, op cit, para 62, pp13 and 14.

62   GLC, op cit, paras B.10.12-B.10.16, p38.

# INDEX

168

171